Heinemann
New Windmills

Stories from Shakespeare

Shakespeare's timeless stories of love, treachery, murder and magic are vividly retold in this collection. Follow:

✦ the gradual descent of a man into evil, as one bloody crime leads to another in *Macbeth*

✦ the strange and magical events in a forest on a Midsummer's night in a *Midsummer Night's Dream*

✦ the treachery that unfolds in Ancient Rome in *Julius Caesar*

✦ the torment of a mad King who disowns the only daughter who is truly loyal to him in *King Lear* . . .

and more . . .

About the Author

Geraldine McCaughrean was born and educated in Enfield, the youngest child of a fireman and a teacher. She worked as a secretary with a television company before studying at Christ Church College of Education. She then had a variety of jobs including editor of a newspaper, literary assistant to the ex-world director of Rothmans and sub-editor in a major publishing company.

Geraldine McCaughrean is now a full-time writer and lives with her husband and daughter, Ailsa, near Newbury, in Berkshire.

GERALDINE McCAUGHREAN

~ *Stories from* ~
SHAKESPEARE

Heinemann
New Windmills

Heinemann is an imprint of Pearson
Education Limited, a company incorporated
in England and Wales, having its registered office
at Edinburgh Gate, Harlow, Essex, CM20 2JE.
Registered company number: 872828

Heinemann is a registered trademark of Pearson Education Limited

09
16

ISBN: 978 0 435125 03 5

Cover illustration by Brian Lee
Cover design by The Point
Typeset by ⊼ Tek-Art, Croydon, Surrey
Printed and bound in China (CTPS/16)

Contents

Introduction

What would Shakespeare think if he could pay a visit to the twentieth century? How would he feel to see his plays in lavish production worldwide, on every bookshelf, included in every school curriculum, if he could see the tourists flocking to his home town, students discussing him on the bus, passers-by quoting him, cinema-goers queueing to see Shakespeare on film, and everywhere his works revered like a second Bible?

In his day things were rather different.

Shakespeare was writing – at speed and in cut-throat competition with a wealth of other good playwrights – for a very demanding audience. If the 'groundlings' in the Globe Theatre, who had paid a farthing to stand and watch, were not enjoying themselves, they would mill about, heckle and throw apple cores. If the gentry grew bored, they would leave. His actors were all men, his plots were all borrowed from other authors, his props and scenery were rudimentary. His sets were even cluttered up with rich members of the audience who would pay to sit on the stage. There were fashions and conventions to be followed – 'mad' scenes were the rage just then – and the latest hit song never went amiss if it could be worked into the action. This week's writing was in next week's repertory.

And yet the plays Shakespeare shaped out of these meagre makings were so remarkable, so complete, and of such universal appeal that four hundred years later the whole world is still enthralled.

Between 1590 and 1612, Shakespeare was coining phrases we are still using today: 'a rose by any other name', 'in my mind's eye', 'be cruel only to be kind', 'beggar'd all description', 'To be or not to be' . . . We quote him every day without even realizing it.

If Shakespeare did 'borrow' his stories, he knew a good story when he saw one, and he knew how to make it better. There is no substitute for seeing the play, nor for reading the glorious language of the poet himself. But here is a glimpse into the variety and excitement of Shakespeare's world. As the Players say in *Hamlet*, you can have whatever takes your fancy: 'tragedy, comedy, history, pastoral, pastoral-comical, historical-pastoral, tragical-historical, tragical-comical-historical-pastoral. . . .' Here are excursions into love, heroism, the supernatural, the bloodthirsty, unbearable sadness and rapturous joy, foolishness and wisdom, faraway places and far-off times. It is a world peopled by the kind of characters you meet in dreams, nightmares or real life. Above all, the plays' chief object was to provide enjoyable, edifying entertainment.

Shakespeare was a man without arrogance or pretensions, a man always glancing over his shoulder at the tide of death rolling in to submerge him. So his greatest pleasure, if he could pay us a visit, would probably not come from glossy fame and adulation. It would come from seeing how, in the end, he tricked death – bought immortality with this extraordinary wealth of words.

Anyone who can do that is well worth getting to know.

The People in the Play

LORD AND LADY MONTAGUE, LORD AND LADY CAPULET,
aristocrats living in Verona whose families hate one
another

ROMEO,
son of the Montagues

JULIET,
daughter of the Capulets

NURSE,
Juliet's old 'nanny' and companion

TYBALT,
Juliet's fiery cousin

MERCUTIO AND BENVOLIO,
friends of Romeo and sworn enemies of the Capulets

ESCALUS,
Prince of Verona

FRIAR LAURENCE,
a monk and Juliet's religious adviser

THE COUNT OF PARIS,
suitor to Juliet

VARIOUS BRAWLING HOTHEADS, CITIZENS, PARTY-GOERS, WATCHMEN

The action takes place in Verona after many years of
petty, inter-family feuding.

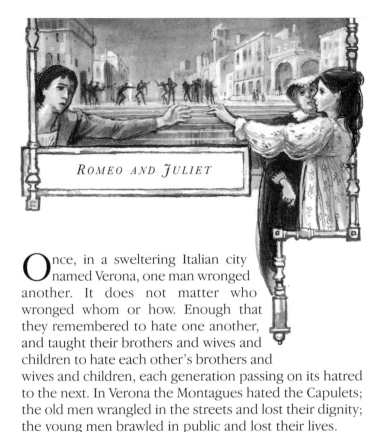

ROMEO AND JULIET

Once, in a sweltering Italian city named Verona, one man wronged another. It does not matter who wronged whom or how. Enough that they remembered to hate one another, and taught their brothers and wives and children to hate each other's brothers and wives and children, each generation passing on its hatred to the next. In Verona the Montagues hated the Capulets; the old men wrangled in the streets and lost their dignity; the young men brawled in public and lost their lives.

Their stupidity infuriated the Duke of Verona. He passed edicts forbidding street affrays. The Montagues and Capulets bowed meek heads in front of him and swore things would be different in future, but inwardly they merely postponed their feud to a later date.

Young Romeo was a Montague, so he and his friends naturally hated the Capulets. They welcomed the smallest opportunity for a fight. And when they were not fighting, they were falling in love.

Romeo was forever falling in love – with a desperate

fervour, though rarely for more than a week. His friends Benvolio and Mercutio were used to it. But on the subject of the latest, 'divine Rosaline', Romeo was in danger of becoming a bore. He moped and sighed about the place and declared himself at death's door because Rosaline did not return his love.

To cheer him up, Benvolio and Mercutio dragged him along to a party at the Capulet house. The fact that everyone wore carnival masks enabled them to gatecrash with ease, and it seemed clever to filch Capulet food and get merry on Capulet wine. The intention was that Romeo should see some new face to take his mind off Rosaline's. In the event, his well-meaning friends were to regret their success. For the face Romeo saw was that of Juliet, daughter of the Capulets. She was fourteen and extremely beautiful.

All Romeo's adolescent crushes, all his imaginary excursions into love, crumbled to nothing. They had all been rehearsals for this: love at first sight, love given and received in a single meeting of eyes. Without even knowing each other's name, Romeo and Juliet fell in love. As their fingers intertwined, so did their lives.

With a flurry of ruffled feathers, the Montague intruders were spotted. Juliet's cousin Tybalt would gladly have run his sword through Romeo then and there, but for the laws of hospitality and the Duke's edict. As it was, he swore to cross swords with Romeo at the very next opportunity. Romeo was oblivious of the vexation he was causing. He left the house . . . but could not leave its grounds; the presence of Juliet held him there, like the cord which ties a hawk to the falconer's wrist. He waited under her balcony for a glimpse of her, and was rewarded by hearing her speak his name over and over – 'Romeo! Romeo!' – struggling to come to terms with loving a Montague.

He spoke to her out of the darkness, and climbed up to

steal a kiss. There was no shyness between them, no elaborate courtship. Time was too pressing and the danger of being discovered too great. It was Juliet who proposed they marry next day. No one else in the world must know, except for the Friar who was to marry them and the go-between by whom Juliet sent word of where and when.

The go-between was Juliet's old Nurse, a jolly, rollicking woman as devoted to Juliet as mother and friend rolled together. During her long life she had seen love in all its guises, and was still as melted and moved by it as a young girl. With her help, Juliet was able to arrange to meet Romeo at Friar Laurence's cell in the monastery, where both were in the habit of going to confession.

The Friar himself was touched with the same fond, sentimental faith in the power of love as the Nurse. He agreed to perform the marriage, hoping that in some way it might put an end to the families' feuding. It would call for careful timing, though, to break the news that a Montague had secretly married a Capulet.

Whistling and dancing with his shadow across Verona's marketplace, the blissfully happy Romeo overtook his friends Mercutio and Benvolio. He was in love with the whole world. Suddenly, though, his shadow collided with another – that of Juliet's cousin Tybalt, roaring boy and fighting cock of the Capulets. Tybalt was holding a drawn sword.

'I'll teach you to come to a house uninvited, Romeo Montague!'

But Tybalt did not receive the reaction he was expecting. There were no snarled insults, no braggartly threats given in exchange for his.

Romeo said, 'I don't want to fight you, Tybalt. I can't! You would understand if you knew. . . .'

'Oho, I do! You're a coward, I know that! Too scared to

fight!'

'No, Tybalt, on my oath, I . . . I can't explain why, but God knows, I've more cause to love you than hate you this morning.'

'Romeo?' His companion Mercutio was horrified. 'What are you saying? Here's this filthy Capulet calling you out, and you tell him you won't fight with him? Well, if you won't, I will!'

'No, you don't understand, Mercutio.'

But Mercutio's sword was already drawn. If Romeo would not fight, then he would have to defend the honour of the Montagues himself. He was too disgusted with Romeo to pay him any more attention, and Tybalt was in no mood to listen either. Though Romeo ducked and dodged between them, pleaded with them to put up their swords, the blades clashed and the curses flew. Romeo dived between them and restrained Mercutio's sword arm. Tybalt seized the opportunity to lunge. The blade passed under Romeo's arm and pierced Mercutio in the heart. His dearest friend died in Romeo's arms, cursing Montagues and Capulets alike.

Blinded with rage, Romeo snatched out his sword and ran Tybalt through – forgetting Juliet, forgetting the edict, forgetting what a price there would be to pay.

Already the alarm bells were ringing; the city guard were on their way. Nothing remained but to run or face arrest. Romeo fled to the monastery, and there Friar Laurence brought him the news – that he was banished from Verona for ever.

'Leave Verona? Leave Juliet? I'd sooner the Duke had condemned me to death!'

Friar Laurence told him off roundly for such a foolish, defeatist attitude, and dispatched him to visit Juliet one last time before fleeing the city.

Romeo hardly dared face her. Meeting the old Nurse,

he found her bitterly grieved by Tybalt's death. She had always adored the boy – the whole family had. Now all her bawdy jokes were extinguished, her face grown as grey as her hair. And if the Nurse was so very altered by grief, Juliet too might have changed.

'Does Juliet hate me for killing her cousin?'

'She hardly knows which to cry about more – Tybalt's death or your banishment,' said the Nurse, her eyes cold and embittered.

But once they were together, Romeo and Juliet rebuilt heaven out of the ruins of the day. One night was theirs before Romeo was obliged to flee the city or die. But it was a long, sweet night, which increased their love still further. One life was ending, but another would soon begin for them, outside Verona. Once reunited, they would rely solely on each other for their future happiness.

So Juliet's parents, visiting her bedroom a few moments after Romeo's departure, seemed like intruders, strangers. 'Your father, my dear, has arranged a day of happiness to mend all your heartache over Tybalt's death,' said Juliet's mother. 'Next Thursday morning – just a couple of days from now, my goodness! – the Count of Paris will be waiting at the Church of Saint Peter's to make you his bride. There now! What do you say to that!'

'I say he shan't . . . I mean he can't. . . . No! Never! It's not possible!'

Her parents' indulgent faces froze over. They called her ungrateful, wilful, obstinate. When she dared not explain herself, her father flew into a rage and told her she *would* marry the Count or be turned out of the house, disowned.

In her desperation, Juliet ran to Friar Laurence. 'What shall I do? I'm already married to Romeo! I'd sooner die than marry Paris!'

'Die? Yes . . .' mused the Friar. 'And so you shall, my

child – or something like it – if you have the courage to do as I say.' He gave her a potion whose effect would be to suppress all signs of life, without actually killing her. 'Go home and tell your parents you are ready and content to marry the Count of Paris. Then, on Wednesday night, drink this potion. Your parents will come to wake you for your wedding, and – God pity them! – think you dead. Your body will be carried on an open bier through the city – as Tybalt's was today – to the Capulet vault in the churchyard, and laid among your ancestors. I'll send word to Romeo to come at once. He'll be there at your side when you wake, and you can leave the city together. The world's larger than Verona, you know. There must be room in it somewhere for true lovers to be together.'

This time Juliet could not even confide in her Nurse. The contents of the bottle terrified her. She drank deeply, even so. The shriek that went up in that bedroom next morning echoed through the streets and set all the starlings circling in a black cloud over the city. For Juliet lay on her bed cold, white and still, with no more sign of life than her cousin Tybalt when he was carried home from the marketplace. Friar Laurence heard the weeping and comforted the distraught parents. But *he* did not weep. He congratulated himself that there was a letter even then speeding along the road towards Mantua, where Romeo sat waiting for news. It explained everything – the potion, the reason for it, the need for Romeo to return at once, in secret, and keep vigil in the tomb beside his sleeping wife.

But the letter went astray. The messengers carrying it were detained by a plague scare on the road to Mantua, and the first and only message to reach Romeo was of Juliet's death. Nothing of the plot, the rendezvous or the remedy.

He bought poison and rode back to Verona as fast as his

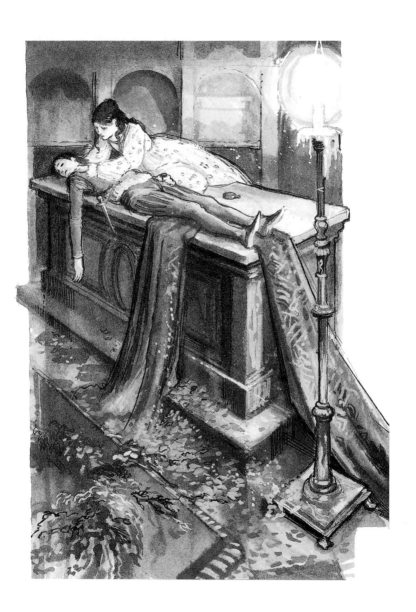

horse would carry him. He found what he had no reason to disbelieve: the corpse of Juliet lying in her family's tomb. It was the work of a moment to drink down the poison and set off in pursuit of Juliet's soul on the starry climb to heaven.

When Juliet awoke, she found Romeo lying by her side. His body was still a little warm from life, but touched by icy death. 'What, didn't you leave one drop for me?' she said reproachfully, holding up the empty poison bottle. Then she drew his dagger and quickly sank it in her heart; there were voices and footsteps outside, and she had no wish to be stopped in her pursuit of Romeo.

Friar Laurence would surely have done better to tell the truth, to have spoken up and said, 'Juliet can't marry Paris. She is already married – to a Montague.' But though he was cowardly and misguided in what he did, he proved right about one thing. The love of Romeo for Juliet *did* unite their families – not in the joys of a wedding but in their inconsolable grief.

As they stood in that vault and saw Juliet, lost to them twice over, and Romeo, banished not from Verona this time but from the earth, their grief was too deep for thoughts of vendetta. Montague and Capulet shook hands in a pledge of peace. But the hands they clasped felt already as dusty and frail as those of the skeletons who watched from the shadowy shelves of the Capulet tomb.

The People in the Play

CHORUS, OR COMMENTATOR,
setting the scene

HENRY THE FIFTH (1387–1422),
newly crowned King of England

VARIOUS DUKES, EARLS AND CHURCH MINISTERS

CHARLES THE SIXTH,
King of France

CATHERINE,
his daughter

THE DAUPHIN,
his arrogant son

MONTJOY,
a French herald and diplomat

THE FRENCH GENTRY

OFFICERS, SOLDIERS AND BOYS IN HENRY'S ARMY

PISTOL, NYM, BARDOLPH,
once companions of Henry, now soldiers of fortune

The action follows Henry's invasion of France in 1415 to
settle ownership of disputed territories.

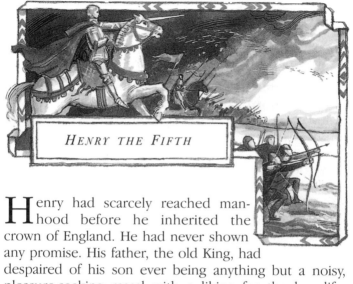

Henry had scarcely reached manhood before he inherited the crown of England. He had never shown any promise. His father, the old King, had despaired of his son ever being anything but a noisy, pleasure-seeking rascal with a liking for the low life. Now, all of a sudden, he was obliged to rule a country, take charge of a government, take on the solemnity and demeanour of a king. Few thought he could do it.

For one thing, there were so many people ready to take advantage of his youth: his old drinking cronies, his ministers seeking to advance their careers, his country's enemies. No sooner was the crown on his head than his advisers were urging him to make war on France and reclaim lands filched from the English. Smug, dusty lawyers presented him with screeds of complicated evidence, thinking to baffle him with legal jargon. But Henry cut simply through their entanglements of words. 'Just tell me – can I justly lay claim to the lands?'

They had thought he would leap at the chance to declare war, almost for the sport of it. But Henry knew better. He knew war was no game but a fearful final resort, and was not prepared to embroil his country in a struggle for land unless that land was indisputably his. He was even prepared to hear the French side of the argument, and ordered, 'Send in the French ambassador!'

The ambassador came not from the King of France but from his son, the Dauphin – an arrogant, preening, sarcastic young man hardly older than Henry but who believed himself ten times better.

'The Dauphin sends this treasure chest,' said the ambassador, 'and trusts it will compensate Your Majesty for those pieces of France you wanted for your playground but may not have.'

'What is the treasure?' asked Henry. The little chest was solemnly unlocked and the lid thrown grandly back. . . .

'*Tennis balls?*' Henry only narrowly curbed his temper. 'Please thank the Dauphin and tell him, when I come to France I shall give him a game of tennis which will knock his father's crown out of court. This insult has decided me upon war. Doubtless that war will kill men, women and children by the thousand. Let us see if this joke of his still raises a laugh in France when the widows and mothers run sobbing across blood-soaked battlefields!'

The ambassador took two steps back, open-mouthed. Was this the rowdy, good-for-nothing waster, the delinquent disappointment of his father, the unpromising newcomer to England's throne?

Thus the English flags were raised and men rallied to them out of every shire and town. Good men, brave men, honest men. Cowards, liars and rogues. Englishmen, Irishmen, Scots and Welshmen. Fluellen and Williams, Bates, Court and McMorris, veterans and boys scarcely old enough to know why or where they were going, all took sail for France in a flurry of fists, oaths and bad jokes.

Bardolph, Nym and Pistol, three drunkards who had known King Henry when he was plain 'Prince Harry' and accounted him their friend, drank deep to old companions then reeled aboard the boats to make what profit they could from the war. Some go to war for the cause, some for the glory, some for the loot, some because they have nothing better to do, some because they have nothing worse.

The English stormed into France and forged a path through the countryside as far as Harfleur. They swept against the city walls like waves breaking against a cliff – as if they would hack the very stones apart with their pikes. At each charge, there in their midst, sword upraised and bare-headed, King Harry galloped on a snow-white charger. His voice boomed above the noise of the battle and put heart into every man who heard it, for he seemed to prize all men equally be they yeomen, ploughmen or knights of the realm. He made them all feel like heroes and the sons of kings, and when he stopped speaking they could barely hear the mines exploding beneath the walls of Harfleur for the beating of their proud English hearts. They hurled themselves through the gaps in the broken wall, while, high overhead, the French watched in vain for the Dauphin's reinforcements. After three or four onslaughts, the city surrendered.

But it did not suffer the usual fate of captured cities; no blood-letting, no rape. Harry gave orders that the townspeople were to be treated with honour and compassion, forbidding a rout. And when they marched away, the English traversed the countryside, by order of the King, as meek as a flock of lambs, paying for their food and leaving the villages along the way unmolested. Henry's was to be an 'honourable' war. Instead of looting, the infantry contented itself with throwing harmless insults at one another like rotten tomatoes, at the same time enjoying that fierce camaraderie only soldiers-in-arms achieve.

Bardolph discovered to his cost what Henry meant by 'honourable' war when he stole from a church. He was hanged for it – strung up from a tree by order of his one-time drinking companion, King Harry. He was left dangling from a noose for the crows to peck at, his life no more to Henry than a dishonourable stain on the name of England.

Harfleur had taken its toll. There were injuries, losses. Disease and fatigue infiltrated the English camp, weakening and dispiriting the men. The weather turned foul.

France stirred itself. The English were faltering on their route march, and France mustered, at last, a far larger army. The French counts and dukes blustered. The Dauphin champed at the bit in his eagerness to be killing Englishmen. The French ladies raised their eyebrows and asked, 'What manner of men *are* these English lions?' to taunt their lovers. Even the royal Princess Catherine expressed a sudden interest in the English language and set about learning it – an idle game to pass the time.

When the Dauphin's ambassador came once more to the English army mired in muddy fields near Agincourt, it was to threaten sudden slaughter. Henry openly admitted that his army was tired and sick – unready and unfit to fight. 'But you may tell the Dauphin that if he comes, we shall fight him as we are, and as we are we shall defeat him!'

Grand words. But what went through Harry's mind the night before the battle? Not for him the sleep of the ordinary soldier, who does what he is told without asking why. Here were his subjects, his children, and the responsibility of their lives weighed heavily on him. He fell on his knees and prayed, 'Oh God! Don't punish past sins tomorrow with the deaths of these innocent men!'

Across the lightless gulf between the two encamped armies, the noise of the enemy came drifting on the wind. The French knights were laughing, gambling, boasting, drinking, as confident of victory as men can be who outnumber the opposition five to one. Their shadows moved giant-like across the panels of candlelit pavilions.

In the English camp there was no heady excitement, no eagerness for morning. Fluellen picked a fight with Williams, and swore to settle with him after the battle; it was a way of pretending they would both still be alive. Most just sat about, thinking of wives and families, of what kind of deaths they might die on a muddy field, trampled and broken. Harry moved among them, cheering them, greeting them by name, joking with them – anything, just as long as they felt his presence there, sharing the same darkness. Later, he pulled on a borrowed cloak and walked anonymously among the camp fires, to glean the true thoughts of his men. He heard many good things of himself. But he heard other things too, things men would never have dared speak to the King's face.

'Halt! Who goes there?' They were nervous.

'A friend,' said King Henry.

'Whose regiment?'

'Sir Thomas Erpingham's.'

The soldier relaxed. 'And how does Sir Thomas feel about this battle tomorrow?'

'Like a piece of driftwood on a beach, waiting to be washed off by the next tide,' replied Henry, knowing it was true.

'I bet he doesn't say as much to the King.'

'No, but I dare say the King has his own misgivings, same as any other man. Don't you think?' Henry ventured.

'It's all right for him,' said Williams's voice out of the shadows. 'If he's captured, he'll just pay a ransom and go home. It's death for the likes of us.'

'But the King says he won't be ransomed. I've heard him say it.'

'Oh, he says that now. But who's going to hold him to his word when all our throats are cut?'

'Are you calling me – the King – a liar?' They almost came to blows over it. Then Henry recovered his sense of humour and exchanged gloves with Williams, promising to settle the argument after the battle. In truth, he would rather have exchanged places with the soldier. It was horribly plain to see how these men had entrusted their lives into their King's safe keeping, and held him responsible for everything that happened to them. As day approached, he heard one of his officers mutter, 'If only we could fetch here a tenth of the idle cowards lying in their beds in England right now.'

'Why?' asked Harry, in a voice which carried to the outermost camp fire. 'If we all die, that's quite enough men killed for one day. And if we win, we happy few! Ah! All the more glory for us!' Then he drew them a picture – not of dead Frenchmen or battlefield booty, but of a later time, a time in England when the battle called 'Agincourt' would be remembered like a feast day in the calendar. Every year when that day came round, it would rouse old memories. Veterans of the war would show off their scars and tell their friends about a day of such heroism, such national glory, such unrepeatable grandeur and romance that those who had stayed home would curse themselves for having missed it.

He showed them such love, their Harry, that he gave them someone to die for. He drew such a picture of England that he gave them somewhere to die for. And he gave them such courage that they felt no need to die at all – not until every French soldier was done for! The English were transformed from the sorry wreck of a straggling army into a pack of baying hounds hungry for the hunt.

The longbowmen loosed arrows which fell like teeming rain. And everyone took up the battle cry they had used at Harfleur: 'Harry, England and Saint George!'

Against all rules of war, a French detachment circled the battlefield and slaughtered all the young English boys left guarding the provision wagons. The carnage they left behind evoked such horror, such disgust, even among England's most hardened old soldiers, that they forgot caution, forgot fright, forgot grubby gain and went after the murderers with naked swords. Men like Nym and Pistol waded into the fray despite all their natural cowardice and idleness, so that the French atrocity recoiled on those who had committed it.

By the time the pale sun went down beyond the muddy fields of Agincourt, the surviving French were gaping open-mouthed at their defeat. Their silk-fringed banners covered the dead, their marvellous horses lay butchered, their gilded armour was being filched by scavengers, and kites gathered in the sky, darker than the rain clouds. The victory was England's, against all odds, and the defeated French could think of nothing but negotiating a truce. More than 8500 Frenchmen lay dead, the flower of French nobility. And of the English? Just twenty-nine dead, if the history books are to be believed.

Amazed at still being alive, the English squabblers, braggarts and roaring-boys tumbled off the battlefield and went in search of familiar faces – where's that Irishman, that argumentative Welshman, that talker McMorris, that fool Pistol? Even Williams, when he found he had vowed to box the *King*'s ears, was hardly abashed. 'It's your own fault!' he maintained staunchly. 'If you *will* go around dressed like a common man, you can't blame me if I take offence at you!' (Even so, he did not box the King's ears.)

For Pistol, it was a lousy war. It took his friends – first Bardolph, then Nym, hanged for robbing the dead. And on returning home, he found his wife dead. He resolved to take up petty theft, having less to show for his trip to France than Harry did.

The French countryside was similarly devastated – its menfolk dead, its vines, fields and hedgerows neglected in pursuit of a fruitless war. Not just the French but the whole of nature cried out for peace. It was Princess Catherine who provided the solution. From the moment Harry saw her, he knew that all hopes of peace lay in her. He would marry her and ally the royal houses of England and France. It would be no hardship to marry such a woman for the sake of her country! All that remained was to ask her. For once, however, his rhetoric and pretty phrases failed him. Whatever he said in English the Princess could not understand, and whatever he attempted in French only made her laugh out loud. Still, his clumsy wooing did eventually win Catherine – she even allowed him a kiss to seal the bargain. And with that kiss, the war came to an end.

Henry became a father soon after his marriage, and he died not long afterwards. But he is remembered to this day for a glorious interlude, a valiant enterprise, one rainy day in France when God seemed to fight back-to-back with the English and all His angels shouted, 'God for Harry, England and Saint George!'

The People in the Play

OBERON,
King of the Fairies

TITANIA,
Queen of the Fairies

PUCK,
a mischievous sprite who does Oberon's bidding

PEASEBLOSSOM, MOTH, COBWEB, MUSTARDSEED
AND OTHER FAIRIES,
followers of the quarrelling King and Queen

HERMIA,
who loves Lysander but is betrothed to Demetrius

HELENA,
who loves Demetrius but is not loved in return

LYSANDER AND DEMETRIUS,
rivals for the hand of Hermia

EGEUS,
Hermia's father

NICK BOTTOM, QUINCE, SNUG, FLUTE, SNOUT, STARVELING,
a band of Athenian workmen indulging in amateur
dramatics

THESEUS,
Duke of Athens

HIPPOLYTA,
his wife-to-be

The action takes place on the eve of the Duke's
wedding, in a fairy-filled wood near Athens.

Something was wrong in the world
of fairies. Rain filled the ditches,
swamped the fields, rotted the crops
and ran like tears down the abandoned
village maypole. All this in July. In
Greece! There was discord among
the spirits, a falling out between the
King and Queen of the Fairies over
which of them should have a little
Indian changeling boy for a page. While
they sulked and fumed and stamped their
fairy feet, the rain kept pouring. There was
every chance it would still be raining on
Duke Theseus's wedding day.

   The Duke was due to be married on Midsummer's Day,
and the citizens of Athens could think of little else –
unless it was the weather, or their own dreams of
marriage. Big, buxom Helena dreamed of marrying
Demetrius, but there was no hope of that for Demetrius
was besotted with her friend, little dark-haired Hermia,
and Hermia's father approved. It was all settled. Her

father had told Hermia to marry Demetrius. The fact that Hermia was in love with Lysander was of no importance.

Hermia stood up to her father and refused Demetrius point blank, but was told, 'Marry him or I'll put you in a nunnery and you can go without a husband altogether.' As a result, little Hermia and Lysander took things into their own hands. On Midsummer's Eve, they eloped. They walked off into the forest, determined to be together come what may.

The only person who knew they had gone was Hermia's lifelong friend, Helena. Hoping that such behaviour might change Demetrius's mind about whom he wished to marry, Helena went to Demetrius and told tales. 'Lysander and Hermia have run off together! Didn't I always tell you I loved you more than she did?'

She did not get the reaction she had hoped for. Demetrius promptly drew his sword and strode after the lovers, swearing vengeance on Lysander. Helena was left to stride along behind, reminding him ten times hourly how she loved and adored him. It was not what Demetrius wanted to hear.

'Leave me alone, can't you? I've told you till I'm hoarse, I can't stand the sight of you!'

'And I can't bear to be away from you!' wailed Helena.

They crashed into the forest like a stampede of cattle, disturbing the fairies, whose nerves were already jangled. Oberon, King of the Fairies, and Titania, his Queen, had met by accident in a moonlit glade. Their quarrel had flared up again. After the skirmishing was over, a thousand gossamer wings still trembled with shock in the pallid starlight. Oberon, who had lost the skirmish, decided to punish Titania for again refusing him the Indian boy. He dispatched Puck, his master of mischief, to fetch a certain potent herb for the sake of its magic. . . .

Meanwhile, a group of working men came crashing, like a caravan of donkeys, into the forest glade. They were looking for somewhere quiet to rehearse a play in honour of the Duke's wedding. They had chosen something suitably romantic – the story of Pyramus and Thisbe. In the play, thwarted lovers arrange to meet by moonlight; the fair maiden is frightened off by a lion, and the handsome hero, thinking the lion has eaten her, kills himself. They thought it just the thing for a wedding.

There was Peter Quince the Carpenter, Flute the Bellows-Mender, Snug the Joiner, Starveling the Tailor, and Snout the Tinker. And, of course, there was Nick Bottom the Weaver, whose enthusiasm almost made up for their joint lack of acting skills. What with Bottom, who would have liked to play all the parts himself, Snug, who had no memory for lines, and Flute, who spoke his all-of-a-lump, Peter Quince found directing drama was not as easy as he had first supposed.

While Oberon waited a few minutes for Puck to circle the earth and bring him the magic herb, his peace was shattered by Demetrius, hotly pursued by Helena. Still Helena was protesting her love, and still Demetrius was spurning it. The Fairy King, as he eavesdropped, was moved by Helena's distress. 'I'll soon put this to rights,' he thought.

Then, like a shooting star, Puck returned from his errand – a dart of movement glimpsed in the corner of an eye. Armed with the magical purple-petalled flower, Oberon squeezed some of its juice into the eyes of his sleeping Queen. 'Whatever you see when you open your eyes,' he whispered with malicious pleasure, 'however grotesque, however foul, love it with all your heart and soul. Let it be something *horrible*.' Then, like the spotted snake, he glided silently away . . . and told Puck to do the same for Demetrius – to make him love that big, neglected girl who followed him about.

Unfortunately Puck, not knowing there were two Athenian boys in the grip of midsummer madness, found the wrong twosome, and squeezed the flower into *Lysander*'s eyes.

Helena tripped over her friend's lover in the dark, mistook him for dead, and pummelled at him anxiously until he woke up. So as he opened his eyes, he saw through purple mists . . . a picture of perfection! He leapt up and embraced Helena's knees, pressed his face to her thigh, and begged leave to worship her.

'Oh, how could you!' she cried, stamping on his foot. 'I know it's Hermia you love, but to make fun of me at a time like this!' And having as hot a temper as she had a passion, she stalked off, while Lysander tottered after her, lovestruck.

Hermia, woken by a nightmare and finding herself alone, cast about for her Lysander, calling his name. No answer. What could have happened to him? She rushed into the dark embrace of the wood, as afraid for her lover as for herself.

'Wait behind that bush, Bottom,' said Peter Quince, 'and when you hear your cue, come out and say your lines.'

Bottom picked his way through the brambles, muttering his lines to himself to get them off by heart, and squatted down behind the bush. Spiders and beetles, slow-worms and hedgehogs came trekking by, casting their shadows like outgrown chrysalides. Then Bottom's ears started to itch.

For that master of mischief, Puck, seeing this great gangling lummock littering up the fairy woodland had been too much of a temptation. He had given Bottom the head of a donkey. And when Bottom answered his cue and stepped out from behind the bush, his fellow actors took one look at him, screamed, and fled, with an invisible Puck hard on their heels to chase them through bogs and briars.

'Oh ha ha, very funny,' Bottom called after them loudly. 'Think you'll make an ass out of me, do you, with your fooling about? Well, *I'm* not bothered!' Still, to be alone in the middle of a wood in the middle of the night was a little unnerving, even for a man of Bottom's calibre, and he began singing to raise his spirits.

The particular spirit he raised was Titania, Queen of the Fairies. She opened her eyes, saw the see-sawing, hee-hawing head of a donkey right overhead, and cried, 'O, exquisite creature! Where did you come from? Let me touch you! Tell me your heart's not given to another! Grant me the right to love you, adore you, dote on you!'

The donkey blinked at her, dilating its big, wet nostrils and grinding its yellow teeth. 'Well, I don't rightly know why you'd want to go and do a thing like that,' Bottom drawled. But he did not stop her stroking his ears; it was a very agreeable sensation. Bottom was puzzled to be loved by a fairy but, as with his acting, he had a good enough opinion of himself not to question his luck. When Titania summoned her fairy helpers – Peaseblossom and Moth, Cobweb and Mustardseed – to weave him flower garlands, bring him nectar, and scratch his head, he did not complain about that either.

Puck saw it all and reported back to his master the effects of the purple juice. Oberon was delighted – until two Athenian lovers trailed by again beneath the tree where Oberon sat. Demetrius had briefly shaken off Helena and even managed to find Hermia, his runaway fiancée, wandering alone in the woods. But he was no better off for having found her.

'You've killed him, haven't you!' she greeted him. 'You've killed my darling Lysander while he slept! How

low can a man stoop? Where have you hidden his dear body? Tell me!' Then she ran away from him and instantly and completely lost her way.

'This is the girl I saw,' whispered Puck, 'but not the man.'

'Fool!' said Oberon. 'You've squeezed juice in the wrong pair of eyes, you silly sprite! Go and make amends immediately.' So Puck went and dropped love juice in Demetrius's eyes, as Oberon had originally intended. He even managed to do it just as Helena (with Lysander close behind) caught up with her idol again.

Always unloved before, Helena soon found herself with not one but *two* men mooning after her! Both Demetrius and Lysander, to her total bewilderment, were hurling compliments at her, and dogging her through the woods in hope of a kind word. They did not get one. She naturally assumed they were both making fun of her.

'Everyone knows you love Hermia!' she retorted to Lysander's protestations of love.

'Oh *her*. Demetrius can have *her*.'

'No, no,' said Demetrius. 'I'm quite content. You eloped with her; you have her.'

'No, you! I've found someone far better!' declared Lysander.

Their raised voices guided little lost Hermia into their moonlit clearing.

'She's yours!' Demetrius was shouting.

'No she's not, she's yours!' Lysander shouted back.

'Helena loves *me*, she's always said so!'

'That was before you contracted to marry Hermia.'

'I told you before: leave that minimus out of this!'

Hermia's jaw dropped as she realized that the men were talking about her.

'Oh, you sneak thief! You temptress!' she shrieked, running at Helena and jumping up as if to scratch out her eyes. 'What have you done to them? You've bewitched them! You're trying to steal my Lysander!'

Towering over her, equally angry, Helena retaliated, 'What, you too? Are you going to join in this cruel, wicked joke? After all our childhood years together?' Meanwhile, the rivals in love, Demetrius and Lysander, had their hands on their sword hilts and were starting to talk of 'fighting to the death' for the right to marry Helena.

On a branch overhead, swinging his feet, Puck the mischief-maker looked on in amazement. 'What fools these mortals are!' he whispered to the Fairy King. Oberon kicked him off his perch so that Puck rattled down through the trees like a falling pine cone.

'This is all your doing. Use the love-flower to put things to rights, or by morning we shall have dead Athenians strewn round the wood like dirty washing. Go after them. Roll up the moonlight and paint the night blacker so that they miss each other in the dark. Lead them to opposite ends of the wood where they can't hurt each other. In the meantime, I shall undo the charm on my proud Titania.'

An hour earlier, walking in the wood, the Fairy King had found his Queen busy festooning the donkey-headed Bottom with flowers and jewels. So obsessed was she with her new love that she had lost all interest in the little Indian boy. 'Take him, take him,' she said dreamily, and Oberon had simply carried the boy away. He found his joy in winning marred, however, by the sight of Bottom still being caressed and garlanded. He did not like to admit it, but he was a little jealous of Bottom the Ass.

> *Be as you were*
> *See as you saw.*
> *Fairy awake, and see your mistake.*

With a second, neutralizing flower, Oberon anointed the eyes of his Queen. Flies circled Bottom's long ears and crawled on to the cheek of the Fairy Queen.

It had stopped raining. The fairies no longer wished to be at war. When Titania awoke, the face she saw above her was Oberon's, and she liked the expression in his eye. 'I had the oddest dream,' she murmured. 'I dreamed I was in love with an ass.'

'There's your donkey, beside you,' said Oberon, and Titania gave a shriek of horror at the sight of Bottom, ears a-flop, nose a-flicker, dreaming of oats and carrots. 'Come away,' said her fairy true-love. 'The day's dawning. Away fairies! Away elves and goblins! Let the wood stir and the dew glisten. Let the birds sing and the creatures listen!'

So the day dawned fair after all for Duke Theseus's wedding. The sun shone hot, the wet ground steamed, the weather vanes turned to the west, and the clenched flowers unfolded like fists. Nature and the fairies were at peace once more.

'Helena, I love you,' said Demetrius.

'Who am I to argue?' said Helena.

'Hermia, I love you,' said Lysander.

'I should think so too,' said Hermia.

'At last that's settled,' said Puck, discarding crushed flowers.

He was just wiping his purple-stained fingers through his hair when the ground shook and a clamour of huntsmen galloped into the wood. Demetrius drew Helena close; Lysander shielded Hermia in his arms. But the leading huntsman reined in his horse just in time to avoid them. It was the Duke Theseus, celebrating his wedding day with a dawn hunt.

Behind him rode a dozen Athenian noblemen as well as his African bride-to-be, Hippolyta. Hermia's father was there.

'Hermia? What's the meaning of this!' he demanded. 'I warned you: submit to marriage with Demetrius or be shut up in holy orders! And you, Demetrius . . . is this any way for a betrothed man to behave? Let go of that woman!'

The Duke interrupted him. 'There's a superstition that if unmarried maids or men go walking in the woods on Midsummer's Eve, they'll meet their true-loves. These lovers seem to have done that – and they must have what midsummer gave them. Today in the temple, when Hippolyta and I make our vows, let these couples be married too, and may the fairies bless us all! . . . Thank the gods it's stopped raining.'

'Most fair Pyramus!' A dishevelled workman with straws in his beard stumbled out from behind a bush. The company stared at him and he stared back, clearly expecting someone else.

'What did you say, fellow?'

'That's my line. That's what I have to say when I come on. Must've fell asleep back there. Now I come to remember, I did have the oddest dream. . . .' Bottom's speech petered out. 'My line, sir, for the play, sir. At the wedding. But where did Peter Quince get to?' Bottom scratched his head and found, to his great surprise, a daisy chain over one ear.

The Merry and Regrettable Tragedy of Pyramus and Thisbe was the highlight of the wedding feast. Everyone forgot their lines. The Lion apologized for roaring. The heroine had a three-day growth of beard. The Moon was so burdened down with props that he clattered across the stage like a tinker's handcart, dragging a stuffed dog behind him on a piece of string. The Wall held up two rude fingers to represent a hole, and the hero – 'Now I'll kill myself' – took forty-three lines – 'Now I die!' – to expire – 'Now I am dead!' – after stabbing himself – 'Dead! Dead!' – in the armpit – 'Now my soul has fled!' – with a wooden sword. The audience fell off their benches laughing – which came as a surprise to the actors. But it seemed to suit the Duke very well, for he awarded a purse of gold to every man-jack.

After the brides and bridegrooms, the guests and the actors, the servants and the townspeople had gone to their beds, windows open on a perfect balmy night, Titania and Oberon led their fairy band in and out of the houses. They laid their blessing on every eyelid and on every heart, leaving the silent rhymes of their magic verse written on the moon-white air, like footprints on a fall of summer snow.

The People in the Play

JULIUS CAESAR (c101–44BC),
Emperor of Rome

MARK ANTONY,
his young protégé and a senator

CASSIUS,
a fervent Democrat plotting to murder Caesar

BRUTUS,
his friend and fellow conspirator,
noble in birth and character

PORTIA,
Brutus's wife

CALPHURNIA,
Caesar's wife

OCTAVIUS CAESAR AND LEPIDUS,
joint rulers with Mark Antony after Caesar's death

THE PEOPLE OF ROME

A SOOTHSAYER

VARIOUS SENATORS, CONSPIRATORS, SOLDIERS
AND VICTIMS OF THE MOB

The action takes place chiefly in Rome, ending on a
battlefield near Philippi.

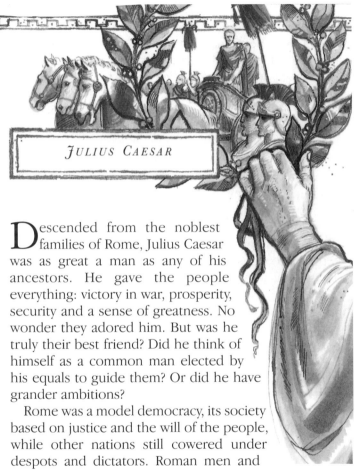

JULIUS CAESAR

Descended from the noblest families of Rome, Julius Caesar was as great a man as any of his ancestors. He gave the people everything: victory in war, prosperity, security and a sense of greatness. No wonder they adored him. But was he truly their best friend? Did he think of himself as a common man elected by his equals to guide them? Or did he have grander ambitions?

Rome was a model democracy, its society based on justice and the will of the people, while other nations still cowered under despots and dictators. Roman men and women were all free and equal, with representatives to uphold their rights in the senate. They had plenty to eat and – thanks to Caesar – plenty of national holidays like today, on which to celebrate their good fortune.

But some saw all that under threat. They regarded Caesar himself as the greatest danger to Rome. 'He towers over the world like a giant, and we creep and peep about between his feet,' hissed Cassius, ripping down the flowers and scarves decorating a statue of Caesar. 'The man wants to be a king, that's what. Wants to make us all back into subjects and serfs.' Cassius was not just some envious peasant jealous of Caesar's wealth. He was an astute politician, a shrewd observer. He did not like what he had seen happening lately in Rome, and he meant to act before it was too late. There were plenty more who felt as he did.

'I see what you're saying, but to kill him! To murder Caesar!' Brutus was slow to be tempted to such wickedness, even by his dearest friend.

'If we don't, he'll put an end to democracy – to everything Rome stands for! It'll be back to despotism, with Caesar ruling like some demi-god, and no one with the power to gainsay him!'

Brutus was a man of the utmost virtue – a close friend of Caesar as well as Cassius – and the notion of a coup horrified him. And yet he knew in his heart of hearts that what Cassius put so bitterly was sadly true. Caesar was a genuinely great man but he did love power; the more he was given, the more he seemed to want. He knew how to get what he wanted, too.

On a recent feast day the people had come herding out to cheer him – his fans, his adoring followers – and offered him a crown of laurels. Three times he turned it down . . . but only with the result that they adored him all the more and clamoured for him to accept the title 'King of Rome' – clamoured, the fools, to give away their rights as citizens of a democracy.

Not Cassius. He believed he could see through Caesar to his true motives, and hated him. Cassius's love was all for Rome and the Roman way of life. No one man must be allowed to harm that. So he set about finding every intellectual in Rome who felt as he did. He needed Brutus more than anyone to join his band of conspirators, for Brutus was respected and loved by everyone. Where Brutus led, others would follow.

Cassius knew his friend was angry, but he was a friend of Caesar too. Besides, anger alone would achieve nothing; was he ready to act? Brutus looked at him long and hard, then nodded his head. He agreed to help kill Caesar. Once convinced of a cause, Brutus was no coward who shrank from acting on his convictions.

As Caesar passed that day through a shadowy archway, a blind fortune-teller sitting in the darkness called out to him: 'Caesar! Beware the ides of March! Beware!' It chilled him to the marrow, that cry. It stayed in his mind, and he was relieved when the fifteenth day of the month – the ides – dawned without incident. His wife had dreamed of murderers lying in wait for him, such fearful dreams that she begged him not to go out. But Caesar was not one to let dreams, or a woman's fretting, unnerve him. Let his enemies read something into the current spate of evil portents and omens; Caesar had nothing to fear. 'Cowards die of fright every day of their lives,' he told his wife. 'A brave man has to face death only once.' So he set off for the Capitol, the city's centre of government. 'The ides have come,' he told the blind fortune-teller blithely as he passed by.

'Yes, but not gone yet,' replied the old man.

The usual enthusiastic crowds surged forward – cheering admirers, people urging their requests on Caesar, senators in their white and purple robes, military men in leather and metal. They jostled and pressed closer, blocking Caesar's way into the Capitol.

Suddenly, naked blades caught the sunlight.

A blow in the back, a sharp pain. Caesar turned to look his assassin in the face: Cassius – gaunt and savage like a jackal. Then a rain of blows followed, delivered by the

whole eager brotherhood of conspirators, a flood of blood and pain. Caesar staggered and reached out for help to his friend, his old friend Brutus. . . . And Brutus struck him a blow which pierced him to the heart, both with its force and for its unforeseen treachery. 'What, even you, Brutus?' Caesar, that legend of an emperor, fell crumpled and limp at their feet.

Afterwards the streets filled with hysterical, terrified citizens. Caesar dead? It was as if the sun had fallen and plunged them into a deep and icy darkness. There was confusion even among the conspirators, a difference of opinion. Should Caesar's bright young protégé, Mark Antony, be killed too? Cassius thought so; he wanted to silence any opposition. But Brutus forbade it. Perhaps if Mark Antony had raged and cursed them and gone for his sword, his death might have seemed necessary. But the young man showed nothing but grief – a touching sorrow at the loss of his great master, but no condemnation of those who had killed him. They watched from a distance as he knelt over the body, ashen and trembling. To have killed him would have turned political assassination into bloody slaughter. Indeed, it was Brutus's avowed intention, if he could, to incorporate Mark Antony's talents into the new government.

At a distance, they did not hear what whispered words Mark Antony dropped into Caesar's ear as he knelt there beside the body. No one heard the oaths, the curses, the vows of vengeance. Docile and respectful, Mark Antony rose to his feet with only one favour to ask of Caesar's killers: that he could deliver the funeral speech in honour of his dead master.

'Don't let him. He'll try to stir up the people against us,' urged Cassius. But Brutus could see no harm, provided he himself spoke first, explaining to the crowds the need for Caesar's death. Brutus was a fine speaker, in the best

traditions of the Roman senate. As the whole populace of
Rome crowded back towards the Capitol, huddling
together for reassurance, Brutus mounted the rostrum
and spoke to them.

'I loved Caesar. No one man here loved him more. Why
did I kill him, then? Because I loved Rome better. He was
my friend; because of that, I weep for him. He was a
triumphant hero; because of that, I honour him. But he
was too ambitious, and because of that, I killed him –
because I love Rome and everything it stands for. The
moment my death serves Rome as well as Caesar's did
today, I am ready to die for her.'

He put it simply, so that the simplest man there could
understand him. The crowds liked that. They had always
liked Brutus – so honest, so honourable. And what he
said made each man proud to be a Roman – a free
democrat and a Roman! The assassination was forgiven by
the time Brutus stepped down. It seemed as if democracy
had been saved by the sacrifice of a single life. The people
of Rome had a new hero – Brutus. 'Brutus for emperor!
Hail Brutus! A crown for Brutus! Hurrah!'

Brutus quietened their cheers, begging them not to carry
him triumphant through the streets but to stay and see
Caesar laid to rest with due respect. He asked them to lend
a patient ear to Mark Antony. They were none too willing at
first. 'He'd better not attack Brutus! We won't hear one
word against Brutus!' they warned, already in the throes of
a new hero-worship. Whatever could Mark Antony find to
say in defence of a would-be despot? Nothing, surely,
without being shouted down and jeered out of town. They
would listen to him because Brutus had asked them to, but,
looking back, the criminal ambition of Caesar was plain to
see. And Mark Antony was no orator – he said so himself.

He said this very eloquently. He put so elegantly the
respect he had for Brutus. He phrased so poignantly

the facts of Caesar's death, showing the body, pointing out which particular wound each conspirator had made. He explained so clearly the need for Caesar to die, returning again and again to the honourable nature of Brutus . . . until it began to sound ridiculous: 'But of *course* Brutus is an *honourable* man!' An honourable man who stabs his best friend because the friend dares to be great, valiant, heroic, splendid, *popular*? Lastly Mark Antony gave them all reasons afresh to love Caesar, reading out from the dead man's will how he had bequeathed money and private land to his beloved Romans.

Like hot metal, he forged them. Like straw, he kindled them. In swearing that he understood and forgave the assassination, Mark Antony managed to make it sound incomprehensible, unforgivable. Taking Brutus's words, he rephrased them until they sounded as damning as any criminal's confession. Like dogs, he incited the crowds to howl and scream for blood. And then he unleashed them. As Caesar's funeral broke up into mob riot, Mark Antony smiled a bitter smile more knowing than had ever lit the face of Brutus – honest, honourable, naïve Brutus.

The violence of the mob splashed the streets of Rome with blood. Anyone and everyone connected with the conspiracy was butchered. Innocent bystanders were hacked to pieces. Cassius and Brutus fled the city. While Mark Antony formed shrewd political alliances, the Roman countryside was plunged into bloody civil war.

So it was that the will of the people of Rome earned them the rulers they deserved: a three-man dictatorship comprising Mark Antony, Octavius Caesar (Caesar's adopted son) and a military man named Lepidus. Between them they drew up a death-list of enemies and undesirables, pricking through the name of each man they believed stood in their way. Hundreds of names were on the list – including, of course, those of Brutus and the detested Cassius.

Outwitted and outmanoeuvred, Cassius and Brutus were still able to muster an army out of the men included on that list. They would fight the new rulers. The odds were against them, but they had nothing more to lose, after all. Everything Cassius had dreaded had come about. Brutus's wife, Portia, had killed herself in despair. Hundreds of their friends had been put to death. But such mutual griefs bound the two men in a greater friendship than ever. There was no more bickering between them, no more disagreements. Together they would see it through to the bitter end – and with honour, too. Perhaps they would even defeat Mark Antony.

After a blood-red sunset, a purple evening settled over the plains of Philippi. On either side of the plain, opposing armies lay encamped, awaiting battle. The candle in Brutus's tent guttered, and it seemed that the tent flap lifted.

'Who's there? What are you?' he called.

'The ghost of Caesar, Brutus, and you shall see me again, I swear it. Tomorrow at Philippi.'

'Till tomorrow, then, Caesar, at Philippi,' said Brutus, and felt a clamminess which was not so much fear as the nearness of death.

Neither side had any real interest in talking. The time for speech-making had passed with the funeral of Caesar. Battle was inevitable. Brutus and Cassius said goodbye to each other – either until the battle was won, or for ever.

And though battle closed around them with its usual senseless confusion and turmoil, the two men, upright as twin towers, held their ground. When each was convinced that defeat was certain, he gave his sword-hilt into the hands of a trusted friend and ran on to the blade.

A single wound from the same blade that had stabbed Caesar. A sharp pain. An end.

'The last of all the Romans,' Brutus said of Cassius before he died. 'Rome will never see his like again.' Then a ghostly figure, purple-robed and king-like, beckoned him from out of the smoke of battle, like an old friend.

Mark Antony paused in his triumph to look down at the body of Brutus. 'All the other conspirators acted out of envy. Only this man acted out of a love for the people. He was a man of real virtue, a gentle man. Oh, such a man.' No one contradicted him, neither the dead nor the living, because some lives speak for themselves without need of eloquent obituary or funeral oration.

The People in the Play

THE GHOST OF MURDERED KING HAMLET OF DENMARK

CLAUDIUS,
his brother and murderer, now King

GERTRUDE,
widow of the dead King, now married to Claudius

HAMLET,
Prince of Denmark, discontented son of
Gertrude and the dead King

OPHELIA,
his sweetheart

LAERTES,
her brother

POLONIUS,
long-winded Lord Chamberlain, father of
Ophelia and Laertes

HORATIO,
Hamlet's closest friend

A TROOP OF STROLLING PLAYERS

A GRAVEDIGGER

VARIOUS GUARDS, COURTIERS, SAILORS AND SOLDIERS

The action takes place around and within the castle of
Elsinore, in Denmark.

HAMLET

There was once a castle full of shadows. They barred the windows, waited on the stairs. Like webs, they rounded the corners of rooms. Like bad dreams, they mustered in the bed hangings and consorted behind the fire's flickering. The king who lived there feasted every night, with fireworks and loud music, but the dark was not dispersed, nor the icy silence shattered. Shadows also circled the eyes of the guests. The ghost which then appeared walking the battlements seemed terrifying to those who saw it, but truly it was only one more strand of the sad darkness.

The guard told Prince Hamlet of the ghost, and he hurried to the roof to see if it would show itself to him. It came. And it turned on him so unmistakable a face that he pursued it across the rooftops, along the frost-caked walls, demanding that it should speak. For it was the ghost of his father, the old King!

'Yes, I am your father's spirit, doomed to walk the frozen nights because I died without time for holy absolution of my sins. Death came too suddenly.'

'The snake bite, you mean?' said Hamlet.

'A bite from the very snake who now wears my crown and sleeps with my wife. . . . Oh yes, Hamlet. My own brother murdered me – poured poison into my ear as I slept in the orchard, to rob me of throne and queen.'

'I knew it! In my soul I knew it!' cried Hamlet, who had never understood why he so detested Claudius. Now he knew why it had appalled him that his mother had married her husband's own brother, and so soon after the old King's death. Murder, of course! It explained all the revulsion he felt for the man who now shared his mother Queen Gertrude's bed.

'Avenge my foul murder!' demanded the ghost. 'And *remember me!*'

'Remember you? Oh God!' How could he not? Hamlet vowed to put everything else out of mind until Claudius was dead. Though he was a young man in love, his plans to marry the Lady Ophelia must wait. Happiness must give way to duty, the duty to avenge his father!

But to conceal his intentions, he would first pretend to be mad – a babbling idiot, crazed by melancholy. Claudius would think himself safe then, and Hamlet would have no difficulty in killing him. It would not be hard to feign madness; Hamlet felt half-mad already, hatred and horror pounding at him like a black sea. He told his best friend Horatio what he was planning, but the fewer people who knew, the better.

He might have confided in his dear Ophelia. But suddenly Ophelia had become cold towards him, had said that she could no longer return his love. Hamlet could make no sense of her unkindness. He was not to know it was her father's doing – her domineering, insensitive father Polonius, putting a stop to the love affair. Ophelia now looked to Hamlet like one of the enemy, not to be trusted with his awful secret.

So Ophelia was terrified next day when her former sweetheart, dressed all in black, came lurching into her room, wildly dishevelled, and raved at her like a madman. With her brother Laertes newly set sail for France, whom could she run to but her father?

Pompous, windy old Polonius was no longer the wise politician and philosopher he had once been, though he still held his position at court. He sometimes made wrong decisions now, and would talk in platitudes rather than think. Still, Ophelia loved him and told him everything that had happened.

'Have you spoken unkindly to the Prince lately?' he asked.

'I did as you commanded me,' said Ophelia helplessly. 'I told him I couldn't see him any more.'

'Ah! Then that's what's driven him mad!' said Polonius confidently. 'I thought he was toying with your affections; that's why I told you to give him no more encouragement! But he was clearly in love with you after all! Well, well.'

And that was what he told King Claudius and Queen Gertrude when, to their horror, they also witnessed Hamlet's hysterical behaviour, his gibberish, his wild-eyed excitement.

'You'll see. You'll see. It's disappointed love at the root of this,' Polonius assured them. 'You must hide behind one of the tapestries in the long corridor, and I'll arrange for the youngsters to meet there by accident,' he continued. 'You'll see! It's love! I should never have interfered!'

Love. Too powerful a force to interfere with.

Madness. Too dangerous a disguise to wear.

Hamlet's lunacy may have begun as a pretence, but given the events of the last few days, he was no longer fully in command of his wits.

Hamlet was a student and a thinker. By choice, he would have left Castle Elsinore at the same time as Laertes, to further his studies, but his doting mother would not let him go. The ghost insisted that he stay. So his scholarly brain had nothing to exercise it, no questions to tax his intellect, to puzzle over and wrestle with, except for the problem of how and when to kill Claudius. He turned the facts over and over, looking at them from every angle.

Suppose the ghost had been a demon sent from hell to trick Hamlet and tempt him into committing a damnable sin? Suppose there was no truth in its story of poisoning? It had to be considered. Hamlet needed more proof. He needed to think.

But the deeper he thought, the deeper Hamlet sank into depression and despair. His father was murdered; his perfect mother was not so very perfect after all; Ophelia no longer loved him. Was such a life really worth living? Was *any* life? Just then, suicide seemed to Hamlet the sensible choice of any sane man – if it were not for the fear of some after-life worse than the present one. That was all that goaded men on, day by intolerable day – the terror of something worse if they lay down and slept the sleep of death

While Hamlet pondered suicide, Polonius, King Claudius and the Queen were hiding behind the hangings in the long corridor, anxious to convince themselves, by spying on him, that Prince Hamlet was indeed mad for love of Ophelia. If that was his problem, then everything was easily put to rights. Polonius instructed his daughter to stroll along the corridor.

'Hush! The Prince!' hissed Polonius excitedly.

Coming unexpectedly upon Ophelia in the long corridor, Hamlet was caught off-guard by her fragile beauty. He nearly dropped his pretence of madness.

. . . But when all she wanted of him was to return his gifts and love letters, his bitterness returned in double measure. And then – worse – it suddenly occurred to him that there were eavesdroppers listening. His heart fairly broke.

'Where's your father? At home? Tell him to stay there, then, and keep his doors locked at night! And you – become a nun, why don't you? Why would you want to have babies and bring more sinners into the world than there are already?' To think that she had conspired against him with his enemies! He ranted at her, pushed and harangued her, maddened by despair.

After he had gone, the eavesdroppers emerged from their hiding-place shaken but unsure what to think. Gertrude was aflutter with anxiety. Claudius felt threatened, however, and determined to send Hamlet out of the country as soon as possible. Polonius blundered on with his wishful thinking, babbling of disappointed love. But Ophelia, standing forgotten and overlooked, simply grieved for Hamlet's sake, that such a fine mind should have been lost to ugly madness.

Having thought and reasoned and argued himself to a standstill, Hamlet found himself incapable of doing anything. Then a chance arrival at the palace spurred him to action. A band of strolling players, who visited Elsinore every year, shattered its suffocating silence, spilling colour into the grey courtyards with their gaudy costumes and bawdy clowning. Their especial talent with tragedy gave Hamlet an idea. He took the player-manager aside and instructed him to perform a particular play in front of the royal family: *The Murder of Gonzago*. A slight addition to the script, a small adjustment to the plot, and there it was: the story of a king murdered in an orchard by a devilish brother, for the sake of crown and queen. The players performed it that same evening. As the filthy

murderer emptied his vial of poison into the ear of the sleeping Gonzago, Claudius lunged out of his chair and fled the room, shouting, 'More light! Give me more light!' His hands plucked at the air as though a black net had snared and enveloped him. Hamlet had his proof: Claudius was guilty.

But Claudius now realized that Hamlet knew about the murder. He must be got rid of. The King gave orders for the Prince to be put aboard ship and sent at once to England.

Meanwhile, the Queen summoned Hamlet to her bedroom to demand an explanation of his outrageous behaviour. Exultant to the point of hysteria, Hamlet raged unrepentant into his mother's room.

'Hamlet, you have upset your father very much,' said Gertrude.

'Mother, *you* have upset *my* father very much!' he retaliated.

'Hamlet! Remember to whom you are speaking!'

'How could I forget? You're the Queen, aren't you? Your husband's brother's wife and – more's the pity – my mother!' In his mind's eye, Gertrude's willingness to marry Claudius made her almost as guilty as her murdering husband. He was so agitated that Gertrude feared for her life. 'Help!' she shrieked, and someone behind the tapestry shouted out as well.

Without hesitation, Hamlet drew his sword and drove it through the tapestry, thinking to kill the King where he stood. But it was not Claudius. It was Polonius – meddlesome, interfering old Polonius. Hamlet could barely spare the emotional energy to regret his terrible mistake. Instead he continued to reproach his mother, so convincingly that he almost won her round to his point of view. She might have become his ally – had he not suddenly looked up and seen again the ghost of his father.

Gertrude saw no ghost, no ghastly, armoured spirit. She saw only the empty air and concluded that her son was stark mad.

'What are you doing, Hamlet?' moaned the ghost. 'Why are you here? Did I send you to torment your mother? Did I ask you to take vengeance on her? Leave her be! Remember the real villain! Remember the vow you made to avenge me!'

Hamlet tried to make his mother see the ghost, but it was no use. He was filled with remorse for failing his ghostly father. But now his hopes of killing Claudius were overshadowed. His sword had pierced the wrong heart – killed an innocent old man – and he could not evade the palace guards for long. His passage was booked on a ship to England. There seemed every possibility that Hamlet's chances of revenge were gone for ever.

Claudius certainly meant to leave nothing to chance. Entrusting Hamlet into the custody of so-called 'friends', he wrote a letter for them to carry with them, a sealed letter of introduction to the King of England. The letter read: *'This man Hamlet is an enemy of the state of Denmark. Kill him.'*

Claudius was thwarted, however. Pirates attacked the ship carrying Hamlet to England. The Prince alone was taken prisoner and, on payment of a ransom, returned to Denmark. He sent letters ahead of him – to his friend Horatio, to his mother and (recklessly) to the King. He came back altered, calmed, and with a sense of proportion born of seeing the world's far bigger troubles. On the borders of Denmark he had watched twenty thousand men preparing to do battle over a patch of worthless ground. What was so burdensome about Hamlet's fate alongside such senseless waste?

The death of Polonius, however, had had devastating consequences. His daughter Ophelia, already steeped in misery over Hamlet's madness, ran mad with grief herself. She sang doleful songs of the graveyard, and doled out flowers to anyone who would take them from her, smiling the wistful, witless smile of a madwoman.

Polonius's son Laertes, learning of his father's murder (without hearing who had done it), returned to Denmark crazed with fury. He found the country on the verge of rebellion, bewildered at the death of Polonius, and led the rabble to the palace. It was all Claudius could do to stay alive long enough to explain. Laertes's sword was at his throat.

'It was Hamlet who killed your father, not me!' he gasped. 'That madman, Hamlet! Calm yourself. Be patient. Do as I say and your father's death won't go unpunished!'

Poor Laertes had no sooner learned this than he was told of his sister's madness. He had no sooner wept at the sight of her – wandering the palace, singing, her hands full of flowers – than Ophelia drowned, like a child, mindless of the river's dangers. Grief upon grievance worked Laertes into a violent passion. Hamlet must pay.

It was at the funeral of Ophelia that they met face to face. Hamlet was passing through the graveyard only by chance, and happened to stop and talk with a gravedigger. Then the dismal little funeral procession wound its way between the headstones – all faces Hamlet knew. There was his mother, in obvious distress, the King – and Laertes too! Who could have died? Hamlet had no idea, until the body was lowered into the grave and Laertes leapt after it for one last embrace of his sweet sister.

'Not *Ophelia*!' cried Hamlet, with sudden, horrific realization. Laertes sprang at him, wrestled with him in the very grave, their boots kicking dirt over the frail white corpse, bruising its fragile white flowers. They fought about who had loved her more, the poor, loveless Ophelia. When they were pulled apart, the Queen was busy making excuses for Hamlet, blaming his madness, and the King was agreeing: 'He is mad, Laertes.'

Only afterwards, in private, did Claudius encourage Laertes to take revenge on Hamlet for his father's and sister's deaths – not in a hot-tempered tussle in the mud, but with planning and forethought. Nothing must be left to chance. This time Hamlet's luck would not hold. Claudius intended to make sure of that.

The King's heralds trumpeted an announcement. The King had made a bet with young Laertes: six horses against six swords that Prince Hamlet could beat Laertes at fencing. A friendly bout, simply to settle a bet! It would distract people's thoughts from recent sad events.

Though Hamlet agreed to the match, a premonition crept over him, as he did so, of something terrible about to happen. His friend Horatio urged him to call off the fight, but Hamlet brushed his misgivings aside. After all, the match was a friendly one, using guarded rapier-points.

'This is the sword without a guard,' Claudius whispered to Laertes. 'This is the one to choose. The point's been dipped in poison, so one nick and he's dead.' Just to make absolutely certain, Claudius also poisoned a cup of wine for Hamlet's 'refreshment'.

The Prince, when he arrived for the fencing match, was calm and courteous, apologizing to Laertes most sincerely for any sorrow he had caused him, and behaving with princely good grace. Gone was the frenzied, resentful malcontent, too angry to live, too scared to die. Laertes might have thought twice about killing such a man, if Claudius had not fanned him to a white heat of hatred.

But Hamlet was an excellent swordsman. He scored the first hit and would not even break off for the drink Claudius offered him. Again, his blunted sword rapped Laertes's jacket, and it seemed that Hamlet was about to win the King's bet for him. Queen Gertrude was delighted and proud, and went to wipe the sweat from Hamlet's forehead. As she stepped down, she raised a cup of wine to her lips: 'A toast to the success of my clever son!'

'Gertrude, don't!' hissed Claudius, but it was too late. The poisoned wine he had prepared for Hamlet slid down the Queen's throat.

Frustrated to the point of desperation, Laertes struck out at Hamlet. Feeling the sting of a naked rapier tip, Hamlet turned on Laertes in real anger. They struggled in an undignified brawl, dropping their swords and recovering them again – except that Hamlet now held the barbed blade and Laertes the covered one. The wound Hamlet dealt Laertes was much deeper than the nick in his own arm. The poison on the blade went straight to Laertes's heart.

And at that moment, the poisoned wine took its deadly course through the Queen's heart. Staggering to her feet, she fell headlong from the platform.

'It's the sight of the blood! The Queen's fainted!' Claudius tried to tell them, but Gertrude had not yet lost the power of speech.

'No, the drink! Oh my dear Hamlet, I'm poisoned!' she whispered, and Hamlet cried out, 'Murder!'

'You are murdered too, Hamlet,' called Laertes, falling to his knees. 'No medicine in the world can save you. The sword's point was poisoned. It's killing you now, just as surely as it's killed me. Forgive me, friend, as I forgive you. It was the King's doing. The King's to blame.'

Without pause for thought, Hamlet sank his sword's point deep in the King's chest, then forced the last drops of poisoned wine down his throat. Hamlet's revenge for his father's death was complete, though many more crimes had been added to Claudius's charge since that first murder in the orchard.

Few who had lived through those terrible days now survived to say what they had seen. Those who did survive, like Horatio, found so little left in the world of any worth that they would have abandoned it willingly. But, as Hamlet told Horatio with his dying breath, the world needs witnesses to give a true account of its evils and its merits. The dead cannot testify.

The People in the Play

VIOLA,
a shipwrecked girl later disguised as CESARIO

SEBASTIAN,
her twin brother, also shipwrecked

ANTONIO,
a sea captain, who befriends Sebastian

ORSINO,
Duke of Illyria

OLIVIA,
a Countess in mourning, loved by Orsino

SIR TOBY BELCH,
her dissolute uncle

SIR ANDREW AGUECHEEK,
Sir Toby's stooge and hopeless suitor to Olivia

MALVOLIO,
Olivia's self-important steward

MARIA,
Olivia's maid

VARIOUS SAILORS, MUSICIANS AND HOUSEHOLD STAFF

The action takes place after a shipwreck on the
coast of Illyria.

TWELFTH NIGHT

Along the coastline of Illyria – or Albania as it is now – there were often storms: electric storms, thunderstorms, storms of temper, storms of passion. Antonio, captain of the *Duodecimus*, knew it all too well, for he had once fought the Illyrian fleet offshore and was a wanted man thereabouts. He would have steered well clear, if a storm had not wrecked the *Duodecimus* on the beaches. It was a nightmare, that storm – passengers flung into the sea, the ship breaking up around them, the lights of Illyrian houses twinkling above the white crashing of water on the rocks. That pretty young girl Viola drowned. . . .

'I don't recommend the place, Sebastian,' he told the girl's twin brother, 'but if your heart's set on looking around, who am I to stop you? Let's go. And don't worry about your sister. I'm sure she's safe somewhere, same as we are.' Sebastian welcomed the reassurance. Antonio was just sorry he could not believe it himself. 'Look. Here's my money. You can't visit a place without a few coins to spend.' And he pressed all he had into Sebastian's hand. The warmest friendships are often born out of calamity.

In fact, Antonio was wrong in thinking Viola drowned. Despite her woman's clothing and the pounding waves, she *had* reached land. Just as she herself was thought to be dead, she imagined that her fellow passengers had drowned, including her dear brother Sebastian. Now she found herself alone on a strange Mediterranean shore – no place for a refined nobleman's daughter. So she decided to dress as a boy, call herself 'Cesario' and apply for a post as page at the villa of Duke Orsino, ruler of Illyria.

There were at least two great houses on the clifftop overlooking the sea. One belonged to Duke Orsino. Another neighbouring villa housed the Lady Olivia. Now, as Viola quickly found out, Orsino was in love with Olivia, in love with the very *thought* of Olivia, but most of all in love with love itself. He revelled in it, sweet agony that it was – for Olivia gave him no encouragement at all. On the contrary, Olivia had sworn to mourn for seven years, in tragic solitude, the death of her brother.

Undaunted, the very first task the Duke gave Viola (or rather 'Cesario') was to visit Olivia with a mouthful of poetry to pour in her ear. Viola did not want to go. She did not want the Duke to be in love with Olivia. To her chagrin, she found she was in love with the Duke herself! But she went to Olivia's villa – how could she refuse? – and what a houseful of oddities she found there!

It was not an easy place in which to mourn in tragic solitude, what with Orsino sending love tokens every hour of the day, and a motley household racketing about the house and gardens. Olivia's uncle, Sir Toby Belch, lodged with her. He was not much given to tragic solitude. In fact, if he had ever met it, he would probably have knocked it on the head, tucked in his napkin, taken up a knife and eaten it, washing it down with a good wine before falling asleep with his face in it. Opinions of him were mixed: Olivia was fond of him, in a despairing kind of way; Maria the maid adored him; and Malvolio the steward detested him. The visiting Sir Andrew Aguecheek looked up to him (except when Sir Toby fell down drunk, of course, when Sir Andrew generally tripped over him).

Sir Andrew had hopes of marrying the Lady Olivia. Sir Toby had planted these hopes, so as to tap all the money out of Sir Andrew's purse on the pretext of helping him win her. You might almost have felt sorry for Sir Andrew, fooled and fleeced out of his gold, if it were not for the man's quite groundless vanity. Only Malvolio, the pompous, lugubrious steward of the house, made Sir Andrew look good by comparison.

As mistress of such a household, the Lady Olivia stood out like a swan among ducks. Viola was immediately struck by her beauty – but not as stricken, unfortunately, as Olivia was by 'Cesario'. The lady's resolve to live sad and alone wavered then and there. 'Tell Orsino I can never return his love,' she said. 'Tell him not to bother sending any more messengers . . . unless perhaps it's *you*.'

Viola left, torn between joy and sorrow that Orsino could never win his beloved Olivia. But before she reached the gate, Malvolio came lumbering after her. 'My mistress sends back your ring. Don't want it. Won't keep it. Sends it back.' And he dropped a ring on the ground.

'But I never gave her any ring! I. . . . Oh *no!*'

The dreadful truth dawned on Viola. The Lady Olivia was in love with *her*! Poor soul! It seemed as if everyone in Illyria was doomed to unrequited love: Sir Andrew, the Duke, Olivia, and Viola herself. And soon even Malvolio was to join the ranks of the broken-hearted.

Malvolio was making life a misery below stairs at Lady Olivia's house. He stalked the servants' quarters as if he were lord and master. He preached and pontificated. He bullied and blustered. He disapproved loud and long of Sir Toby and Sir Andrew. When they rolled in at two in the morning, roaring and reeling, crowing like cocks and swapping bad jokes at the tops of their voices, Malvolio came down and delivered them a sermon like a broadside of cannon.

Sir Toby belched in his face. 'D'you really think 'cos you're a sobersides, the rest of the world's going to stop enjoying itself?' Malvolio stalked away, vowing to report them to the mistress, chased upstairs by gales of beery laughter. But his tirade had soured the night's fun. Proud Malvolio was ripe for a fall. And if anyone could give him a helping push, Maria the maid was the girl to do it.

Walking next day in the grounds of the villa, Malvolio found a note written in handwriting remarkably like Lady Olivia's – a love letter, surely! The writer was clearly urging some secret admirer, in code, to declare himself: *'even though you are below me in rank . . . M—O—A—I, these letters rule my heart!'*

'All those letters are in *my* name!' cried Malvolio. 'My lady loves *me*! And why not? I've known all along I was meant for great things – wealth, glory. . . . Now let me see. What is it I have to do to show I've understood her? Wear yellow stockings, yes. Cross-garters, yes. . . .' He read on, believing what he chose to believe, oblivious of the giggling behind the hedge and of the possibility that someone was playing a trick on him.

Viola did her utmost to persuade the Duke that his suit was hopeless, to give up, to love elsewhere. But Orsino showed no sign of relenting. You might almost have felt sorry for him if it were not for his pig-headedness. Instead he sent her, like a lamb to the slaughter, straight back to Olivia's open arms and adoring eyes.

Veiled in black, and sighing, the Lady Olivia walked her garden in a turmoil of emotions. It did not help her peace of mind when Malvolio suddenly pounced from behind a bush, plumed like a pheasant and with scarlet garters criss-crossing bright yellow stockings. He flourished his hat in her face, giggling maniacally, burbling about 'letters' and 'greatness' and obeying her every fancy. She was so worried by this apparent mental collapse that she summoned her servants to take charge of him. Eagerly, they did so. Olivia did not see with what relish they dragged Malvolio away, or where they took him; she had other things on her mind.

If only Viola had admitted earlier to being a girl! But she had left it too late – if she said anything now, Olivia would be horribly humiliated. 'Cesario' did his best to explain that he could not return the lady's love, but Olivia was not listening, did not want to hear. You might almost have felt sorry for her, if it were not for that obstinate deafness of hers. The situation was getting out of hand. The lady grew more ardent with every passing moment. 'Cesario' fled those beseeching eyes, those outstretched arms.

'I don't know why I stay around,' sulked Sir Andrew Aguecheek. 'Olivia shows more interest in that pageboy Cesario than she does in me!'

'Well, then, challenge the lad to a duel!' suggested Sir Toby, scenting a day's fun. 'I'll deliver the challenge.' And before Sir Andrew could find an excuse, there he was, committed to a sword-fight with his rival in love, 'Cesario'.

'Fight me?' shrieked Viola when Sir Toby delivered the challenge. 'But I've never done the gentleman wrong! Can't you tell him I'm sorry?'

'Only blood will satisfy him,' lied Sir Toby ferociously. 'He's a great sword-fighter, that Sir Andrew.'

'Tell him I won't fight!' begged Viola. 'I'm not man enough!'

'The lad's eager and waiting,' Sir Toby told Sir Andrew. 'Says he'll chop you in pieces.'

'Oh mercy me! Gracious! Heavens! You mean he likes a fight?'

'Nothing better. Killed a dozen men that way, I hear tell.'

Tirelessly, Toby Belch worked away on the two innocents, persuading them they had to fight each other. Both were terrified, so there was no real danger of anyone getting hurt. It was a bit of harmless fun.

Still, Viola could not tell the difference between a coward and a killer. So she fled those bloodshot eyes, that outstretched sword. . . . Then, all of a sudden, up stepped a stranger and offered to fight on her behalf. She had never laid eyes on him before, and there he was, ready to lay down his life for her. Fortunately, he did not get the chance, because the local militia arrived and arrested him for being a pirate.

'I'm sorry, but I'm going to need that money I lent you,' said the stranger to Viola.

'What money? I never saw you before. . . . Of course, I'll give you what I can, but. . . .' The stranger seemed unreasonably bitter – quite outraged, in fact, as he was dragged away by the officers, shouting abuse at the person whom, a moment before, he had drawn his sword to protect! It was all very confusing.

As soon as the officers had gone, Sir Andrew, egged on by Sir Toby, went in hot pursuit of his rival in love, content now that 'Cesario' was feeble enough to bludgeon.

Meanwhile, close by, the Lady Olivia, in search of her darling 'Cesario', found him right outside her gate. She smiled, and touched, and gazed with such adoring eyes that 'Cesario' allowed himself to be drawn indoors out of the day's heat. . . .

Except that it was not 'Cesario' at all. It was Sebastian, Viola's twin brother. Unaware that his kind companion Antonio had been arrested, or that his sister was enmeshed in a series of terrible misunderstandings, a more bewildered boy never set foot in Illyria.

Nor had a more baffled suitor than Malvolio ever banged his head against a brick wall. Locked in a pitch-dark room, treated like a madman, and taunted through the bars of his cell, Malvolio raged and howled like a chained dog. The scarlet cross-garters holding up his yellow stockings cut off the circulation to his feet.

In the morning his hopes and dreams had lifted him half as high as the sun. By evening he lay humiliated, incarcerated, and in pain and half-convinced himself that he was mad. What other explanation was there for the love letter, the brutality, the spiteful voices at the window?

Sebastian emerged from Olivia's house still bewildered, but engaged to be married. He was sorry his good friend Antonio was not on hand so that he could tell him how this perfectly delightful woman had offered her undying love and virtually begged him to marry her. She had everything: money, beauty, rank. And although he had never laid eyes on her before, it felt as if the marriage had always been meant. Who was he to defy destiny? If only his sister could have been alive to see it!

It was at the trial of Antonio, captain of the wrecked *Duodecimus*, that everything became clear. The arrested captain was brought before Duke Orsino in the town centre, charged with piracy, which he vigorously denied. Viola was there at the Duke's side once more, in her role of 'Cesario'. The captain began to rage at the sight of her, calling her an ungrateful traitor: 'I rescued that boy from the sea myself – saved his life! I looked after him and served him these three months past! Then, when I come to his aid, at danger to myself, as you can plainly see, he refuses even to know me!'

'But this boy has been in *my* service for the last three months,' said the Duke. 'So you must be lying. . . .'

A flurry of movement, a rustle of silk. The Lady Olivia, no longer in mourning, came half-dancing through the afternoon shadows. The sight of her robbed Orsino of all self-control. Her casual rejection of his love and her obvious fondness for 'Cesario' pitched him into a violent rage. 'I've loved this boy, God knows, past all reason!' he cried, grasping Viola round the neck. 'But since he's clearly the one you love most in all the world, why don't I just kill him here and now to spite you?' He did not mean it, of course, but Viola was almost sorry he let go; she would gladly have lain down and died for her beloved Duke.

'Where are you going, Cesario dearest?' asked Olivia.

'After my dear Orsino, whom I shall always love better than anyone in the whole world,' said Viola candidly.

Then it was the Lady's turn to rage. 'What, love him better than me? Have you forgotten your vows so soon? Is this how a husband treats his wife?' she wailed.

'*Husband?*'

She even brought out the priest to prove it: Olivia had just now married her 'Cesario'. That little piece of news set the Duke shouting again, so that presently Viola was being savaged by both a jealous Duke and an aggrieved 'wife'.

This was the moment Sir Andrew and Sir Toby chose to stagger into sight, clutching their heads and yowling. 'He hit us! He hurt us! That Cesario! Made us think he was a coward, and all the time he was a vicious brute of . . . .'

'Cesario did?'

All eyes turned on Viola. She tried to deny it. She swore she had never done anyone the smallest harm in her life. Who knows what might have happened next if a new face had not come along. It was Sebastian.

'I'm sorry, dearest, I'm afraid I've injured some of your household,' said the newcomer to Olivia, sheathing a bloody sword. 'But believe me, I was provoked.'

They stared at Sebastian.

They stared at Viola.

Their eyes travelled to and fro like shuttlecocks.

Viola stared at her twin brother and he stared at her.

'There were two of them all along,' said Sir Andrew, rubbing his broken head.

'So when you kept saying you loved me . . .' said Orsino.

'I meant every word,' said Viola, and the Duke understood why he had always felt such a very strong regard for his little pageboy.

When she realized her mistake, the Lady Olivia had no wish to undo it. And Sebastian certainly did not. It was as if he had stepped into a dream of both a dead sister and a new wife, and had not been required to wake.

Malvolio emerged from his underground cell as if from a nightmare. Everybody laughed to see him dirty and dishevelled, his yellow stockings dangling and even his hair trembling with rage. 'I'll be revenged on the whole pack of you!' he bellowed, but they only laughed all the more.

You might have felt sorry for him if it were not for his ridiculous pomposity. No. No matter what his faults, you could not have helped feeling sorry for him. Almost.

The People in the Play

OTHELLO,
a Moorish nobleman and general in the Venetian army

DESDEMONA,
his bride

BRABANZIO,
a senator and Desdemona's father

THE DUKE OF VENICE

IAGO,
Othello's jealous, scheming henchman

EMILIA,
Iago's wife

MICHAEL CASSIO,
Othello's handsome lieutenant

BIANCA,
Cassio's mistress in Cyprus

RODERIGO,
a Venetian gentleman in love with Desdemona

VARIOUS SENATORS, SAILORS, SOLDIERS AND GENTLEMEN

The action begins in Venice and continues in a sea
port on the island of Cyprus.

OTHELLO

The name Othello was on everyone's lips. Othello: hero of the
wars, leader of men, general and
diplomat, the pride of Venice. His
troops would have gone to hell
and back for him. The Venetian
parliament was undyingly grateful.
Tonight Venice had great need of
such a man. Tomorrow Othello must
depart on an urgent mission.

So the great and busy men of state
did not want to hear him attacked,
accused, abused, especially by a fellow
senator. They tried hard to pacify the old
man storming up and down the assembly room,
ranting of wickedness and witchcraft. 'I tell you he's
married my daughter! Don't you understand?' wailed
Brabanzio. 'The man's a sorcerer and a devil. He must
have used some filthy potion to bewitch my
Desdemona!'

'But we thought Othello was a dear friend of yours!'
said a bewildered senator.

'So he is! Was! But would you let your daughter marry him? Eh? A Moor? A man old enough to be her father? I'd sooner that fool Roderigo had had her!'

For any man to discover that his daughter has just married in secret, without his blessing, without his permission, without even a word, is a terrible blow. When she has been as dear as Desdemona was to Brabanzio, the shock is even worse. Nothing but witchcraft could explain such behaviour to Brabanzio.

His complaints were holding up the vital business of parliament. But they had to be answered. When Othello arrived he was immediately called to account. 'What have you to say, Othello, to the accusation that you have enticed away Desdemona with witchcraft?'

Brabanzio seethed. 'What can he say? Do you really think a quiet, gentle girl like my Desdemona would choose to marry *him*?'

'Ask her. Send for her,' said Othello calmly. 'And if she says I married her against her will, let me die for the crime. I'm just a soldier. I'm not clever with words. All I can do is tell you how our love came about. My friend Brabanzio here used to invite me home often. I'd start recounting old campaigns and adventures of mine – shipwrecks and sieges; horses charging into the smoke of battle; banners and faces painted with glory – that manner of thing. Desdemona would creep in, quiet as a mouse, and sit listening. She'd gasp and sigh and laugh – sometimes she'd even cry at the stories I told. Then one day she whispered that if I had a friend like me who loved her, I should tell him not to keep silent out of shyness. I took that for a hint. I admitted to loving her. That, gentlemen, is the sum of witchcraft used.'

'Liar!' Still Brabanzio raged and ranted.

So Desdemona was sent for, and answered her father's accusations with the same calm composure as Othello.

'Until today, I owed all my love, obedience and respect to you, Papa. But here's my husband, and now we're married my life belongs first and foremost to him.'

Brabanzio threw up his hands in despair. At once, all his bitterness was transferred to his daughter. 'Watch her, Othello! When she eloped with you tonight, she deceived me. Doubtless she'll do the same to you.'

The senators of Venice smiled and nodded at the married couple, happy that the 'unpleasantness' had been sorted out. In truth, they could spare the matter no more time. The Turkish fleet was advancing on the island of Cyprus! For a city like Venice, dependent on shipping for its livelihood, it would be a disaster for the enemy to seize such a crucial stronghold; from there they might take control of the whole Mediterranean. So Othello must set sail for Cyprus at once – tonight – and fortify the island against attack. In private the bigoted senators might sniff at the thought of a white girl marrying a black man. But when it came to fighting a war, what did it matter what colour the general was?

'Let me go with him,' said Desdemona. 'Tonight should have been our wedding night. If Othello sails for Cyprus, how can I bear to stay here in Venice without him?'

'Just as you like.' The senators bent over their maps. Their minds were already taken up with more pressing affairs.

There was someone other than Brabanzio who believed his heart broken by the marriage. Roderigo – one of the sillier knights to board ship for Cyprus that day – had mooned for many months after the lovely Desdemona, only to see her lost to Othello.

'Lost? She's not lost, man! It's just a matter of time till she gets tired of seeing his ugly face in bed beside her,' said Roderigo's good friend Iago. 'Trust me. I'll soon have you in Desdemona's arms, you see if I don't.' Trust Iago? Why not? Everyone trusted honest Iago.

Othello himself trusted him. He did not realize that Iago called him names behind his back, hated him with an insane loathing, blamed him for a dozen imaginary wrongs, and was plotting his downfall. He could not possibly know – being a man of simple virtue himself – that Iago's brain was a dark, contorted place full of wickedness. Yes, Othello trusted Iago.

Roderigo trusted him, too. But poor Roderigo was only Iago's source of ready money. Iago fooled and bamboozled Roderigo, without any serious intention of helping the silly young knight win Desdemona. But then, Iago liked to make use of people, to turn them to his advantage. He had similar plans for Cassio.

Lieutenant Michael Cassio, with his pretty face and fancy manners, was loathsome to Iago. Promoted over Iago's head, Cassio nevertheless looked on Iago as a friend. His heart was also a little saddened by Desdemona's marriage, for he thought her (in his words) 'an exquisite jewel'. But he was more easily comforted than Roderigo; plenty of other ladies adored him for his Venetian good looks.

A fortuitous storm scattered the Turkish fleet. For a few nerve-racking hours it seemed as if Othello might be lost at sea, but the battered Venetian fleet finally docked in Cyprus. The islanders were still in a state of terror; they needed reassurance. Othello's most urgent priority was to restore calm.

Iago knew that, when he got Michael Cassio drunk.

It was not difficult – Cassio could not hold his drink and needed only a glass or two to grow fighting mad. Gullible Roderigo was easily persuaded by Iago to pick a fight with him, and the two came to blows in the middle of the street. The whole town was woken by the noise, and Othello came running with his sword drawn.

'What's the meaning of this? Drunken brawling in the streets? Michael Cassio, you're a good friend but after this you're no officer of mine. I can't rely on a drunkard.'

Cassio was devastated – his career ended, his reputation lost. He wept on the first shoulder offered him. 'Oh God, Iago! My reputation! Gone for ever!'

'Is that all? Well, that's no great loss,' snorted Iago. 'But if you really want your job back, why not ask Desdemona to help you? Othello can't refuse her the smallest favour, and she's always ready to help a friend in trouble.'

'You're right! I'll do it! I'll ask the exquisite Desdemona to speak to Othello on my behalf! What a good friend you are, Iago!'

Iago smiled his villainous, deceitful smile. Everything was going just as he had planned. All that remained was for Iago to bring Othello home nicely on cue – just as Cassio was leaving Desdemona's side.

'Wasn't that Cassio, talking to my wife?' asked Othello casually.

'No, surely not! Why would he sneak off guiltily when he saw you coming?' Like a gardener pushing a seed into fertile earth, Iago planted in Othello's brain the first small seed of suspicion, the tiniest germ of anxiety.

Desdemona greeted Othello in a flurry of excitement, begging a favour for an old friend, wheedling and coaxing so playfully that she laughed him into granting it. But the favour was to reinstate Michael Cassio. Afterwards, the look on Iago's face, his anxious tutting, suggested that something was not quite right about that. Othello grew irritated and demanded that Iago speak his mind directly. Iago only frowned and said he was sure there was nothing to worry about.

He played Othello like a fish on a hook, reeling him in, then loosening off the line. He dared not speak his mind, he said. What if he was horribly mistaken? He gave the impression that he hated to talk ill of his fellow man. Then he allowed Othello to wring the 'truth' from him.

'Beware of jealousy, won't you, my lord?' said Iago at last. 'It's a terrible affliction.'

At first, Othello refused to believe anything bad of his wife. Because she was beautiful, did it mean she was unfaithful? No! . . . And yet every time he spoke to her, she chivvied him about Michael Cassio, pleading for him to be given back his post. Othello refused to believe anything sinful could lie hidden inside such perfect beauty. And yet, as Iago reminded him, 'She deceived her father when she ran away with you.'

Othello determined that, if Desdemona did have a lover, he would cast her off sooner than share her with another man. Then he saw her coming towards him with her waiting woman, Emilia. And all his doubts seemed to wash away in a flood of tenderness. He took her hand.

But was it hot from the grip of another man? Was it? His head ached; so many thoughts, imaginings, fears. Desdemona tried to bind his head with her handkerchief, but he pushed it away and the cloth fluttered to the ground. Its red embroidery, bright as drops of blood, caught the eye of Emilia, Iago's wife.

When his wife showed him the handkerchief, Iago snatched it from her with the utmost glee. Time and again he had asked her to steal it, but Emilia would not stoop to theft. She had only brought it to him now in a sad little effort to please an unkind and surly husband. As soon as he took it from her, she regretted doing so.

'You're planning something wicked, aren't you?' Emilia panicked. 'Give it back. My lady will be so upset when she can't find it. It was the first present Othello ever gave her.' But Iago stuffed the handkerchief deep inside his

jacket. He had a use for it. This was to be his 'proof' of Desdemona's unfaithfulness.

'You saw Cassio wipe his mouth with her handkerchief?' Othello's face was a picture of pain. His soul was corroding within him, eaten away by doubts and uncertainties, all put there by Iago's lies. He cursed Iago – punched and shook him – for daring to slander Desdemona . . . and yet it was Iago he asked to give him proof of her unfaithfulness.

Iago bit his lip. 'Sometimes I think I'm too honest for my own good. But if you must see the proof with your own eyes. . . .'

He showed Othello to a hiding-place from which he could watch, but not hear exactly what was said. Then Iago engaged Cassio in conversation, talking to him about his latest romantic conquest – a Cypriot woman – encouraging from him plenty of lewd gestures and crude grimaces. Along came the woman in question and – wonder of wonders! – produced the distinctive handkerchief then and there! In his humiliating hiding-place, Othello writhed and foamed at the mouth to think that Desdemona had given his love token to her lover Cassio and that he had passed it on to another mistress.

It was as if a vast, immovable mountain, steadfast in the midst of a stormy landscape, had suddenly erupted. For Othello's noble calm concealed a welter of pent-up emotions. Huge, unmanageable passion broke him open now and spilled like molten lava, promising destruction to the surrounding world. The Christianity he had adopted along with citizenship of Venice crumbled away and left him calling on pagan gods. He knelt and vowed to be revenged, and Iago knelt too and vowed to help him.

'Let me hear within three days that Cassio's dead. You are my new Lieutenant,' said Othello.

'My friend is as good as dead,' replied Iago sorrowfully. 'But sir, you will let *her* live, won't you?'

'Damn her! Damn her! Help me think of some fit way to kill the witch!'

Iago's plan was nearing its triumphant conclusion. He knew already that he had robbed Othello of his sleep, his sanity, even his reputation. Visiting dignitaries had seen Othello insult his wife in the open street – even hit her – without the least cause or explanation. Emilia, too, he had called all manner of names, making veiled accusations that she had helped Desdemona's lover come and go. Emilia guessed very well that jealous Othello was the victim of someone's odious mischief, but not for a moment did she suspect her own husband.

Now Iago's snare expanded to encompass the hated Michael Cassio – and Roderigo, who had become a nuisance. Exciting Roderigo's jealousy, Iago persuaded him to lie in ambush for Cassio on a dark night with a drawn sword.

It was a messy, botched affair. Roderigo slashed at Cassio, but the thickness of his coat saved him and he wounded Roderigo in return. Iago leapt in and maimed Cassio in the legs, but then the noise of the injured men's screams brought people running. Iago fled, but dared not leave Roderigo alive to say what he knew.

So Iago returned to mingle with those first on the scene, and made a great show of horror at the sight of Cassio's wounds. He whipped out his sword, and in a semblance of righteous wrath, finished Roderigo where he lay, helpless. 'You inhuman dog, Iago,' were Roderigo's last whispered words.

Meanwhile, in the lamplit peace of Othello's quarters, Desdemona confided her unhappiness to Emilia. She tried to be brave but she was out of her depth, could make no sense of what had happened. She could not even bring herself to repeat the names Othello had called her. Emilia, on the other hand, had a terrible opinion of men, and a roving eye. When they talked about love, Emilia seemed to be talking of something quite different from Desdemona – but then, they were married to two very different men. For sweet, sheltered Desdemona, love was all purity, all faithfulness, all obedience to the one beloved man. The change in Othello terrified her, but she went on loving him despite it. She asked Emilia to spread bridal sheets on the bed, then sent her away and blew out all of the candles but one.

Outside in the street there was mayhem – shouting and recriminations, officers questioning witnesses. Roderigo lay dead, Cassio writhed and clutched at his legs, while the Cypriot woman wailed with grief and Iago whispered to the night-watch that she had done it, she was the murderer.

Indoors, in Desdemona's bedroom, all was silence. Between her wedding sheets, Desdemona had fallen asleep. Even Othello entered quietly, believing himself, by now, an administrator of justice bound to carry out due execution. In pausing to gaze at her pale, sleeping face, he hesitated too long. The ripe moment was lost. He even stooped to kiss her, and she woke. Her fear at the look on his face incited him to violence. He demanded her confession, and all she had to give him was the truth: 'I never loved Cassio! I never gave him any handkerchief! Send for the man and ask him!'

But Othello had heard too much evidence, seen too much proof, to have any doubt remaining. 'I can't. By now, your lover's dead.' When she wept at that, Othello found enough reserves of murderous jealousy to smother her and choke the very life out of her.

Too soon for Othello's choosing, Emilia hammered at the door and disturbed his 'act of justice'. Too soon was the pillow eased from over Desdemona's mouth, for she revived briefly and cried out. Emilia heard her and pushed her way in, cradling Desdemona in her arms until her heart finally stopped.

'I did it! I took my own life!' whispered Desdemona. 'Othello's not to blame.'

After that Emilia pecked at the Moor with her questions and curses till he could barely think, making him recount his wife's unfaithfulness when he least wanted to remember it. 'My husband told you? Iago? May his soul rot one grain a day! He lied!'

Then the others arrived off the street – the visitors, Iago, the night-watch. Thick and fast came Emilia's revelations, now that she had witnesses to hear her. She told of Iago's lies, of the lost handkerchief. Her husband tried to frighten her into keeping silent, but Emilia would not be gagged. Not until Othello had been forced, item by item, to hear the truth did Iago manage to stop his wife's testimony with a knife between her ribs, and flee the room.

'Lay me beside my mistress,' Emilia whispered. 'She never betrayed you, Moor, never. She loved you far too much. With my dying breath I swear it.'

No peace. No peace. They crowded him round with their sighs and groans and gabbling. They even brought the wounded Cassio to flaunt his innocence in Othello's face, and the captured Iago to scorch his eyes with the sight of evil. He would have killed the villain but they disarmed him – the worst meddling of all, for he had pressing need of his sword.

So Othello drew out instead a hidden knife, and he cut

his own throat before their noise, their petty justice or his own appalling guilt could swamp him. 'I loved her too much, that was my crime,' he told them, and fell upon the bed, covering his dead wife with kisses and blood as he died.

Then they remembered, those respectable gentlemen of Venice, what manner of man Othello had been – a man modelled on a grander scale than most, whose passions were proportionately greater, whose fire burned hotter, whose life crashed to its destruction from a far greater height. But all they could do was to vent their dismay on Iago and to torture his body, because he had no soul large enough to find.

The People in the Play

LEAR,
King of Britain

GONERIL,
his eldest daughter

THE DUKE OF ALBANY,
her husband

REGAN,
Lear's second daughter

THE DUKE OF CORNWALL,
her husband

CORDELIA,
Lear's youngest daughter

THE DUKE OF BURGUNDY,
suitor for Cordelia's hand

THE KING OF FRANCE,
who marries Cordelia

THE EARL OF GLOUCESTER AND THE EARL OF KENT,
noblemen loyal to Lear

EDGAR,
Gloucester's son, later disguised as Poor Tom

EDMUND,
Gloucester's illegitimate, treacherous son

THE FOOL,
Lear's court jester and pocket philosopher

VARIOUS OF THE KING'S ENTOURAGE, SOLDIERS AND SERVANTS

The action is set in ancient Britain, and would have been
thought an account of actual historical events.

There was once a king – an old king, the foolish, tired, vain old King of England. Old age had made him weary, and power had been his for so long that he had forgotten what a duty of care it brings with it. One day, he summoned his three daughters, Goneril, Regan and, sweetest of all, Cordelia, and said, 'I am weary. I mean to lay down the burden of rule. I shall therefore divide my kingdom between you, in accordance with your merit as daughters. Tell me each of you: how much do you love me?'

'More than words can say,' declared Goneril. 'More than my eyes, as much as my life, as much as any child ever loved her father!'

'Then to you and your husband, Duke of Albany, I give one third of the kingdom. What about you, Regan?'

'Oh as much as Goneril and more!' cried Regan.

'In that case, I give you and your husband, Duke of Cornwall, a third of my kingdom. Now, my dearest daughter Cordelia. Today you choose which of your royal suitors to marry – the Duke of Burgundy or the King of France. But first let me hear how much you love me.'

He should not have needed to ask; Cordelia had always been the gentlest, most affectionate daughter in all she did. But in his vanity, he pursued his question – 'What have you to say?' – and the answer was not as he expected.

'Nothing, Father,' said Cordelia, unable to lie, or flatter, or exaggerate. Her lifelong devotion must speak her love.

'*Nothing*?'

'Nothing. Except that I love you as much as a daughter should.'

Over the years, Lear's temper had grown huge and unchecked like his vanity, and now he threw a tantrum like a spoiled child.

'So unkind? So heartless? So ungrateful for everything I've done for you? Is this all my own daughter has to say? That she loves me "as much as she should"? Well then, from today you're no daughter of mine!' And he split Cordelia's portion of the kingdom between her fawning, flattering sisters, and banished her without a penny to her name.

'Don't do this, my lord!' protested the splendid Earl of Kent. He was a lifelong friend and servant of the King, but he knew stupidity when he saw it. 'Do you really think Cordelia loves you less because she won't pander to your whims? Then it's time someone told you the truth: you've grown into a foolish, selfish old man!'

The court fell silent, aghast at the Earl's daring, afraid for his life. Would the King turn back from banishing the daughter he had always loved best? Or sacrifice to his temper someone else who loved and cared about him?

'Get out! How dare you! Get out of my sight – out of my kingdom – or die for your treacherous insolence!' spluttered Lear, in a paroxysm of rage.

Before he left, Kent turned on Goneril and Regan and accused them: 'How long before your actions put the lie to all those loving words of yours?' He knew the dangerous stuff they were made of. Kent secretly resolved to disguise himself and stay near the King, for the old man's good, even at peril to his own life.

The Duke of Burgundy, seeing the glorious Princess Cordelia reduced before his eyes to a penniless nobody, speedily withdrew his offer of marriage. Not the French King. With or without a dowry, he could see in Cordelia the qualities her own father could not, and he took her, just as she was, for Queen of France.

'And now I shall put the cares of state behind me,' said Lear, recovering his kingly dignity as he thrust the recent unpleasantness out of his mind. 'I shall reside first with you, Goneril, then with you, Regan. Month by month, you may take turns to house and entertain me and my hundred courtiers.'

'Do take good care of our dear father,' said Cordelia to her sisters, as she sadly left to begin a new life.

'I don't think *you* are quite the person to lecture us in our daughterly duties, do you?' snapped Regan, and withdrew to whisper in a corner with Goneril.

The Earl of Kent was not the only minister of the crown to be shocked by the King's sudden abdication. The Earl of Gloucester also strongly disapproved. But he had troubles of his own to preoccupy him. His son, his own dear Edgar, hated him!

In truth, Gloucester was as mistaken about his son as Lear was about Cordelia. Edgar was a dutiful, gentle, devoted boy. But his half-brother Edmund (always before spurned by his family as a villainous waster) had taken steps to oust his brother from home and inheritance. He meant to blacken Edgar's good name and, once Edgar was out of the way, to take over the role of favourite son.

With great care and cunning, Edmund plotted the downfall of his virtuous brother. He went to their father and suggested that Edgar wanted him dead – wanted his own father killed for the sake of his inheritance! He forged a letter in his brother's handwriting. He even inflicted a wound on his own chest to show old Gloucester. 'You see what he did when I refused to help him murder you!'

So, just as Lear had banished Cordelia, old Gloucester put out word for his own son Edgar's arrest. It was a wintry day when Edgar fled his home, but not as cold as the draughts round Gloucester's heart at the thought of his son's treachery.

'I won't stand for it! Not another day!' shrilled Goneril. 'Those knights of his are drunken hooligans. He mistreats the servants and does nothing but carp and complain. Gives up power, then thinks he can still swagger like a king. Well, he's nothing but an idle, senile waster, and I won't humour him one more day!' Such was Goneril's great love for her father.

She was not the only one taking Lear to task just then. His own jester battened on to him like a biting monkey and nipped him with witty insults until the old man's head spun.

'You're a fool,' said the Fool bluntly.

'Why? Why call me that?'

'Because you can abdicate all your other titles, but you were born a fool, so no one can take that one away from you!'

Fortunately, a gentler, more sympathetic stranger had recently attached himself to the ex-King's company. Of course, Lear did not look at him closely, or he might have recognized his banished minister the Earl of Kent in disguise. But then, Lear was all too easily fooled by outward appearance.

'It simply won't do, Father!' squawked Goneril, meeting him on the stair. 'Old men should be wise. You, you surround yourself with drunken oafs and turn my home into an animal house! Send some of them away – or I'll turn them out myself, do you hear?'

'Darkness and devils!' raged Lear, instantly beside himself with fury. 'I don't have to tolerate this! I've got another daughter, remember! Regan would claw out your eyes with her own nails if she heard you speak to me like that! What madness possessed me when I mistook Cordelia for a worse daughter than you? Come, men! Let's leave this place!' And though Goneril's husband, the Duke of Albany, tried to make amends, there was no pacifying Lear. He stormed out of the castle, sending his new friend on ahead to tell Regan to expect him and his courtiers by nightfall.

Kent did not come back with any message of welcome; in fact, he did not come back at all. Not until Lear reached Regan's castle did he find out what had become of his messenger. There sat Kent in the castle stocks, humiliated like a common criminal. And there to greet Lear were both his queenly daughters. For Goneril had hurried round to Regan's castle to be sure of arriving before the ex-King. She suggested to her sister that Regan treat their father as she had done. Consequently, Regan scarcely gave Lear the welcome he had been expecting: 'Go home with Goneril, Father, and do as she says. Fifty knights is quite enough to have around you.'

'Go back? I'd sooner live out of doors! She's a plague! She's enough to drive a man mad! No, I'll stay here with you, Regan.'

'I don't think so, Father. I wasn't expecting you yet. The house isn't ready. And even if it were, I couldn't think of housing more than twenty-five of your appalling knights.'

Smug and self-assured, the daughters watched their father seethe and writhe in the grip of his own anger. Regan was worse than Goneril, he said. He would go back to Goneril, he said, with fifty men.

'I can't see why you need more than ten. Or five,' said Goneril.

'Or even one,' said Regan.

Lear called on heaven to give him patience, tossed his great head, tore at his white beard, cursed and called down judgement. But the sisters simply folded their hands and pursed their lips. And when, in his rage, Lear stamped away into the wet, swirling darkness, with only Kent and the Fool for company, Regan shut her door against him. There was no shelter for miles around, but she simply said that it would 'teach him a lesson' – as if he were a wilful child and not the one-time King of England.

Regan's castle stood on land adjoining the home of the Earl of Gloucester. He soon became aware of what had happened, and though he might have thought old Lear wrong to abdicate in the first place, still he pitied him such ill-treatment. But the ruthless sisters expressly forbade him to offer the ex-King shelter – or even to speak to him.

Outside on the dark heath, reeling and bellowing like a bull, Lear found himself confronted by the worst elements winter could range against him. He screamed at the rain. He roared at the wind. But though the sky

really did pitch down hail and sleet like punishments from God, truly it was a different storm Lear was grappling with. Inside his head regret, rage and horror swirled about, dismantling his powers of reason, leaving his wits in tatters. On the mud of the heath, the old man slithered closer and closer to the brink of madness.

But then the lightning lit up the world with such bright precision that Lear began to see things in a quite new way. When he met Poor Tom, a mad beggar with barely a stitch of clothing, who lived on mice and frogs and babbled gibberish, it seemed to Lear that he had found a sage, a philosopher.

In truth, he had met Edgar, the runaway. Wrongly accused, and in peril of his life, Gloucester's slandered son had taken on the perfect disguise for eluding capture. For who looks twice at a naked beggar whimpering at the roadside? Who looks into the face of a madman?

Lear did. Craving an explanation for why his world had tumbled around him, Lear listened to 'Poor Tom' as if he held the secrets of the universe: a madman listening to a man pretending to be mad. It was a sad sight to see. In fact it was a sight which saddened the Earl of Gloucester so much that he defied the wicked sisters and opened up an outbuilding on his estate to the ex-King and his companions. Little did he realize that his own son was among them.

Here was stillness after the storm, rest after the wandering. Here were light and warmth. Here were true friends (even though some were in disguise).

Gloucester brought bad news. The sisters' cruelty had grown to new proportions; they were ready now to murder the old father they 'loved' so very much. 'You must get away to Dover,' Gloucester advised Kent. 'The King of France has raised an army to put down these

she-devils. But you must get the old man away to safety.'
So Lear and his motley court trailed out again into the
storm – while Gloucester went home, unwittingly, to a
worse kind of darkness.

Goneril, Regan and the Duke of Cornwall were now
determined to do away with the old regime; to purge
the court of 'Lear's men'. Finding out that Gloucester
had sympathies for the old King, they tied him to a chair,
tormented him, ridiculed him. Finally, they excited each
other to such blood-lust that Cornwall gouged out
Gloucester's eyes one by one. Plunged into agonizing
darkness, the old man screamed out for his son – his
only 'loyal' son, Edmund.

'Why call him?' sneered Regan. 'It was he who marked
you out to us for a traitor.'

At last Gloucester realized how the evil brother had
usurped the good one. Edmund had lied about Edgar,
had made him out to be murderous and loveless when
he was really as loyal a son as any father could wish
for. A pair of eyes was the price it had cost him to see
the truth.

The castle servants proved better men than their
masters that night. One died trying to keep Cornwall's
dagger out of Gloucester's eyes – but not before he had
managed to wound the Earl. Another fetched salve for
Gloucester's empty eye-sockets. A third recruited 'Poor
Tom', the village idiot sheltering in the barn, to guide the
blinded Earl out through the storm and across the heath.

Gloucester wanted nothing but to die. Suicidal with
despair and guilt, he begged 'Poor Tom' to take him to
Dover's high white cliffs where he could throw himself
down. And the idiot 'Tom' seemed to agree.

'Are we there yet?'

'Yes, Ooeee, such a long way down! Everything so tiny
down there. . . .' How well Tom described it – so well

that blind Gloucester could almost see the gulls, the rocks, the precipice, the drop.

'Very good. Leave me. Here's money. Go on. Go.' And the would-be suicide blundered, hands outstretched, over the brink, blessing aloud the son he had so misjudged and wronged. Thud! The ground struck him. Though he was too shaken and bewildered to realize it, he had fallen only a few feet. The cliff Edgar had led him to was no more than a grassy knoll. Gloucester was barely winded, though he could make no sense of why he was alive.

'Not dead?' Gloucester heard footsteps and an unfamiliar voice. 'Fall all that way and live? Amazing! A miracle! I saw it all!'

Adopting yet another character, Edgar walked the few steps to where his father lay and knelt down beside him. 'Are you all right, sir? What was that hideous creature that led you to the cliff-edge? A demon?'

'It must have been!' whispered Gloucester, dazed and amazed. 'How could I know? I have no eyes! But it must have been the Devil who tempts men to despair and kill themselves, against all the laws of God! Well, I've been spared! And from now on, I'll bear anything that comes!'

'That's the way. Patience is everything,' said his rescuer softly. 'And I'll lead you wherever you want to go.'

And that was how patient, wronged Edgar helped his old father survive – first disguised as a madman, then assuming a new role as he lifted Gloucester to his feet unharmed. He fooled him out of despair. He tricked him into accepting his sufferings. But still Edgar kept his identity a secret until the time was ripe to reveal it.

There, at the sea's edge, they met up again with Lear. Poor Lear. His thoughts washed to and fro like the surf, and he drifted in and out of madness, barely able to distinguish between real and unreal. But Kent, Gloucester and the rest brought him safely to the beaches where the French King was landing his army. He had come to wreak vengeance on Goneril and Regan for their crimes. And Cordelia was with him.

She was as tender and loving as ever. She forgave him everything. But Lear could barely believe that he was seeing or touching anything so lovely, could scarcely credit that they were reunited, father and daughter. The storm past, he was at least peaceful, but he was exhausted in both body and soul. Given time, he might, step by step, find a faltering way back into his right mind.

No such storm had washed Goneril and Regan clean, or altered their wickedness. Even Albany could not stomach his wife when her true nature came to light, and Cornwall died of the wound Gloucester's servant had given him. So the predatory sisters, pitiless as spiders, each sought to mate with the only man equal to them in wickedness: Gloucester's conniving son Edmund. In their rivalry they turned their venom on one another, each plotting and scheming to be the only love in Edmund's life.

Their rivalry split their unholy alliance, of course, and weakened the military force that together they could have hurled against the invading French. Even so, their champion, Edmund, scored an early success in the fighting and captured Lear and Cordelia.

Malicious by nature, Edmund was by now infected with the bitter hatred Goneril and Regan felt for their ageing father and virtuous sister. He imprisoned the two in a dungeon of his castle. But they persisted in being happy! Lear and Cordelia seemed to want nothing now but each other, and together they were strong enough to face any hardship. Edmund hated to see their happiness. He sent orders – peevish, wicked orders – for the warder to strangle Cordelia. Perhaps in his heart of hearts Edmund knew that the war was lost and wanted to sour the triumph of the French.

Finally, the fighting turned in favour of the French, and Edgar and Edmund came face to face in mortal combat. The country's destiny depended on that fight, but it was a personal vendetta too. His whole life, Edmund had hated his brother. And yet, from the moment Edgar's sword-point struck him in the chest, all that began to change.

Edmund lived long enough to learn of Kent's exemplary kindness to Lear, of Edgar's loyalty to his father. He was still living when they brought word that Goneril had poisoned Regan then killed herself. The news worked a great change on Edmund. 'Such sins on my conscience. . . . No more!' he gasped. 'Send word . . . don't let them do it! Send word to the castle – to the dungeon! Tell them to set Lear free. Tell the hangman not to . . . not to. . . . There's still time! Tell him my orders are countermanded! Do it! Quickly! You don't understand! I sent word that Cordelia. . . .'

Too late. The executioner had already done his duty. Edmund's change of heart could not stop the noose closing round Cordelia's throat. When the victors reached the dungeons of Edmund's castle, they found only Lear left alive to taste freedom. And what kind of freedom was that? The licence to howl and to curse, the freedom to run mad with grief.

'She's not dead! She's not! Look! Her breath moved this feather! She's alive! Fetch help! . . . No. No don't. Leave her. There's no life. You'll never come back to me, will you, my dearest girl? Never, never, never, never,

never.' And with his understanding intact but his heart broken, Lear died with his daughter in his arms.

The Duke of Albany, who had deserted Lear's enemies in disgust and remorse, took on the crown of England. Gloucester, for all his eyes were gone, lived to see what his son Edgar had done for him. But those were dark days still, with no dazzling new dawn to light the way ahead. What does man find out about himself, after all, when suffering strips him bare? What is he? A candle burning on a rainy night, waiting for the storm to blow it out.

The People in the Play

DUNCAN,
King of Scotland

MALCOLM AND DONALBAIN,
his sons

MACBETH,
a general in the King's army

LADY MACBETH,
his wife

BANQUO,
a fellow general

FLEANCE,
Banquo's son

MACDUFF, AND OTHER SCOTTISH NOBLEMEN

LADY MACDUFF AND ONE OF HER SONS

HECATE,
Queen of Witches

THREE WITCHES

VARIOUS LORDS, OFFICERS, MURDERERS AND SPIRITS

The action takes place in Scotland, dramatizing events
which took place between the years 1040 and 1058.

MACBETH

This is the story of Macbeth, whose name is so unlucky that people avoid speaking it.

It began on the day the wars in Scotland ended – a strange day torn between sunshine and storm. Sudden bleak, black clouds blotted out the light. Two horsemen, heroes of the day's victory, rode towards their homes across a Scottish heath, their horses still bloody from battle. Their names were Macbeth and Banquo, and they were as fine a pair of noblemen as Scotland could lay claim to.

Suddenly they were confronted by moving shapes and the hoot of unearthly laughter. Gnarled, leafless trees catching the wind? No. Witches.

Three hags swayed to the music of their own chanting – the kind of women whose magic used to be blamed each time a pig died in the sty or a sailor drowned at sea.

'Hail Macbeth, Thane of Glamis!' called one.

'You know me?'

'Hail Macbeth, Thane of Cawdor!' called the second.

'Hail King Macbeth!' called the third.

Lord Macbeth drew his cloak closer round him. 'What do you mean, Thane of Cawdor? That's not me. I know the man who holds that title.'

The hags cackled and turned their attentions to the other rider.

'Banquo – you won't be king. But your children will be kings, and their children after them!' Then, like bubbles bursting, they were gone, leaving the two men shaken.

Banquo found the prophecy a thrilling piece of nonsense. He laughed and said Macbeth should look more pleased at the prospect of becoming king. But he did not realize, when he said it, just how strongly the witches' prophecy had stirred his companion.

Hardly was there time to recover before a dispatch rider overtook them with word from Duncan, their noble, victorious King.

'Macbeth of Glamis?' panted the rider. 'I have a message for you! The Thane of Cawdor has proved traitor – allied himself to the enemy! King Duncan has stripped him of his title and wishes you to have it in return for your bravery in the battle today. He sends his greetings and thanks and asks if the new Thane of Cawdor might spare him shelter, food and a bed for the night.'

'The King come to Dunsinane? I'll send word to my wife to prepare a fit welcome,' said Macbeth, greatly flattered. But he could not fail to realize that the witches' first prediction had already come true: he was indeed Thane of Glamis and Cawdor.

No sooner had Lady Macbeth received her husband's letter concerning the King's visit, and outlining the strange events of the day, than she had the whole thing planned. One of the predictions had already come true; tonight presented the perfect opportunity for the other to do the same. King Duncan must die before morning.

Ambition burned white hot in Lady Macbeth. She allowed herself no sentiment, qualms or squeamishness. In her eyes, all that stood between Macbeth and his ambitions were his moral scruples – or his cowardice, as she saw it.

So when Macbeth arrived home, she began to persuade him, to coax and bully him. The perfect chance, she said: fate demanding to be fulfilled. Macbeth had always been an honourable, decent man – the King's sworn servant and a loyal Scotsman – but his wife filled his head with such notions of rank and power that his overheated brain began to play tricks on him. He thought he saw, hanging in mid-air, the vision of a dagger. Its handle invited him to grasp it, to grasp the moment, to grasp the crown.

That night, while King Duncan slept under Macbeth's roof, the very host who should have protected him cut his throat. It was a crime so horrible that the castle itself cried out in its sleep.

It was no sooner done than Macbeth regretted it. But Lady Macbeth showed no such qualms. Impatient with her husband's bungling, she coldly and efficiently returned the bloody murder weapons to the scene of the crime, daubing blood on the sleeping servants to incriminate them. She intended it to look, next morning, as if the King's own sons, Malcolm and Donalbain, had plotted the killing and paid assassins to carry it out.

Not everyone was fooled. Macduff, Thane of Fife, instantly suspected Macbeth's part in the murder. But enough were convinced. After all, young Malcolm stood to inherit the crown from Duncan, and a crown has often been a strong motive for murder.

Banquo had his suspicions too. He had heard the witches' prophecy and seen the change it wrought in

Macbeth. As the slandered princes, Malcolm and Donalbain, fled south into England, and the crown of Scotland was placed on Macbeth's head, Banquo realized just what Macbeth had done to come by it.

As far as Macbeth was concerned, Banquo knew too much. Besides, the witches had said that Banquo's children would be kings. It seemed to Macbeth that the crown was not securely his own until Banquo and his son Fleance had been silenced.

Kings do not have to do their own dirty work, however. There are men who will do anything for a purse of gold. So Macbeth hired two assassins to ambush Banquo and Fleance while they were out riding. As the blood-red sunset washed the turrets of Dunsinane Castle, the assassins returned – but father and son did not.

'You killed him? Banquo's dead?' Macbeth greeted them.

'Dead in a ditch, Your Majesty.'

'And Fleance too?'

'Ah, well – he. . . .'

'You fools! You let him get away! Everything's ruined!'

But the coronation banquet was waiting in the dining hall; there was no time for recriminations. His wife urged Macbeth to behave like a king. 'You've just been crowned, haven't you? You should look cheerful, not sick with worry! Be a man, can't you?'

He tried. When he saw the lords and ministers of state ranged around the great table, just for a moment he did feel all Scotland within his fist. Wait. Where was Macduff, Thane of Fife? Stayed away? Spies must be sent to investigate the man. Loyalty is not a thing to leave to trust.

'Sit down, Your Majesty.'

'Where?' asked Macbeth, for there seemed to be no vacant seat at the table. When he looked at the chair where they pointed, a man slumped over his food suddenly sat up and looked Macbeth in the eye. Blood

was hanging in clots from the scalp where the murderers had split his skull. The face was Banquo's.

'No! Who did this? Whose vile idea of a joke . . .?'

'Did what, Your Majesty?' asked the guests.

'Are you all right, Sire?'

None of them could see it, that horrific sight; he could tell from their faces. No one could see that hideous living corpse – no, not even Lady Macbeth.

'Keep away! I didn't do it! You can't accuse me!' Macbeth shouted at the ghost. 'My hands are clean!'

'The King's not well, my lords,' said Lady Macbeth diplomatically, trying at the same time to silence her husband. 'Perhaps you had better leave him in peace.'

But what peace could there be for Macbeth? There was no going back. He had waded so far out into his sea of blood that he was obliged to go on. Seeing Banquo's ghost had shaken him to the core, and he knew he would never enjoy a moment's rest until he visited the witches on the heath and found out, once and for all, what the future held in store.

In a dark cave, filled with the stench from a bubbling cauldron, the three witches sat making black magic. Flesh from snakes, frogs, bats and worms; organs from dogs, lizards, tigers and murdered men – they all plopped into the stinking brew. And blood, of course, always blood. The night was so thick with sinister magic that Hecate herself, Queen of Witches, joined in preparing the wicked spells.

For all the stink, the crones still sensed when Macbeth was close by – he reeked so of evil. They were expecting him, too. He came ravenous for answers, wanting the darkest secrets from the pit of hell. Accordingly they raised for him apparitions from the seething cauldron, the steam shaping itself first into a visored helmet, then a bloodstained child, then a baby in a crown. The apparitions warned him to beware Macduff. But they urged him to press on along the course he had begun, fearlessly, since no man born of woman would ever kill him, and no rebellion would ever defeat him until the day Birnam Wood marched on the Castle of Dunsinane.

'Well, what wood ever walked, and what man was ever born except by a woman? I am invincible! This is what I came here to hear! Before I go, though. . . .'

'Ask no more,' warned the witches.

'But I must know. The rest is useless without it. Will Banquo's heirs ever be kings now that he's dead? Show me the truth!'

Not one apparition, but eight, came in answer to his demand. They came, conjured from the smoke – seven identical images of crowned boys, and lastly Banquo holding up a mirror in which were reflected countless more sons. The descendants of Banquo would, it seemed, rule over Scotland for centuries.

'Why so miserable, Macbeth?' cackled the witches, and danced for him, a grisly, grinning dance like tormented souls writhing in hellfire. Then they disappeared, as if they had never been.

Outside the cave, horsemen brought Macbeth news: that Macduff had fled to England, to escape the fate of Banquo and to join forces with Malcolm, the dead King's son and rightful heir to the throne. No one any longer suspected Malcolm or his brother Donalbain of murdering their father – not now that Macbeth's true nature was coming to light.

'So! Macduff of Fife has escaped me!' snarled Macbeth. 'But his family shan't! If I can't kill him, I'll do the next best thing. No line of kings will spring from *his* family!' And he sent murderers to Fife Castle – not two this time, but a dozen – to wipe out the whole Macduff household.

They murdered every servant, every guard, every man and woman, Macduff's wife and all her little children.

As Macduff discovered on his arrival in England, Malcolm, the rightful heir to the throne, was as different from Macbeth as heaven is from hell. He had a saintly loathing of his own shortcomings – and no ambition at all to rule Scotland.

But when news came of the slaughter at Fife Castle, peaceable Malcolm was finally stirred to revenge. While Macduff wept distractedly for his butchered wife and babies, Malcolm resolved to march on Scotland immediately, to rescue his country and subjects from the tyranny of foul Macbeth.

Back in Scotland, Lady Macbeth, her life weltering in blood, was fast going mad. At night she walked in her sleep, wringing her hands in an endless nightmare of washing. The murder weapons that had bloodied her hands in the King's bedroom that night had stained her to the very soul. In her mind's eye, the spots were still crimson and indelible on her palms. With the invading army within a day's ride of Dunsinane Castle, she killed herself, crushed by guilt.

Up until that moment, Macbeth had thought he had lost all sense of horror. When they brought him the news, he barely knew how to grieve. And yet he knew that his mainstay was gone, his partner, his confederate. His wife had always told him what to do. With her death, life itself ceased to make any sense.

He could make no sense, either, of the messenger who came running from the battlements. For the fool babbled about trees on the march – about Birnam Wood coming closer by the minute. Though it gave Macbeth a moment's blind panic, there was a perfectly simple explanation. The advancing army from England had cut branches from the forest to conceal their numbers and gain a better element of surprise. By the time they threw aside their branches, there was no time for the occupants of Dunsinane Castle to turn tail and run. They had to stand and fight.

So? What had Macbeth to fear, who could not be killed by any mother's son? He laughed his attackers to scorn. He fought them with the casual arrogance of a man who knows he cannot die. Even when Macduff confronted him, pale with loathing, Macbeth was not so much afraid to fight him as unwilling to spill yet more of the family's blood. The crime at Fife weighed heaviest of all on his conscience.

'Spare yourself the sorrow of crossing swords with me,' he warned Macduff. 'A soothsayer told me I shall never be killed by any man born by woman's labour.'

'Despair, then,' said Macduff. 'I was cut from my mother's body after she died. She played no part in bringing me into the world. Surrender!'

But Macbeth would not surrender, even when he saw how the witches' prophecies had misled and damned him. He threw his shield across his body and fought to the last gasp, to the last hopeless, staggering, weary blow, to the moment when his head was struck from his body.

With the death of Macbeth, Malcolm's inheritance returned to him, and, after him, the crown passed to his kindred's clan, the descendants of Banquo, to reign for generation after generation. All that remained of Macbeth was a name in the history books. It is a name so steeped in blood, evil and bad luck that the superstitious will not speak it out loud even now, ten centuries later.

The People in the Play

THE ISLANDERS
PROSPERO,
the deposed Duke of Milan
MIRANDA,
his daughter, cast away on the island with her father
CALIBAN,
a monster born on the island, Prospero's slave
ARIEL,
an airy spirit once imprisoned on the island, now
earning his freedom by serving Prospero
VARIOUS SPIRITS CONJURED BY PROSPERO'S MAGIC

THE SHIPWRECKED
ANTONIO,
Prospero's brother, who usurped his dukedom
ALONSO, KING OF NAPLES,
who helped him
FERDINAND,
son of King Alonso
SEBASTIAN,
envious brother of Alonso
GONZALO,
an old nobleman of Milan who tried to help Prospero
TRINCULO,
a jester
STEPHANO,
a drunken butler
THE CREW

The action takes place on an enchanted island, twelve
years after Prospero is usurped and cast adrift at sea.

It seemed to Miranda as if she had lived all her life on this lonely little island. Her father, Prospero, had told her differently, but for twelve years this island had been her home and she remembered no other. She recalled the past like a dream, the people like characters in a fairy story. She and her father had been cast adrift in an unseaworthy ship by her uncle Antonio, who wanted to be Duke of Milan in place of Prospero. Alonso, King of Naples, and his brother Sebastian had both helped set the ship adrift. The castaways would certainly have died at sea but for the kindness of an old friend. Gonzalo, at peril to his life, had secretly stocked the ship with food and water. His bravery had undoubtedly saved Prospero and little Miranda. But it was fate which had cast them up on these uninhabited shores.

No, the island was not quite uninhabited. Before Prospero, it had belonged to the witch Sycorax. She it was who had landscaped it with thorn bushes and bent-backed trees, stinking bogs and naked rocks. She it was who had captured spirits of sky and sea, like a great black spider catching flies in her web, and made them serve her as slaves. When one airy spirit defied her, she had pinned him inside a split pine tree to howl his days away in agony. She it was who had left behind, when she died, her grotesque son Caliban, to drag his knuckles around the beaches and thickets of the island.

But Prospero knew magic, too, and the longer he lived in lonely exile, the more he perfected the magic arts. He coloured the island with flowers and grassed over its bare rocks. He hung fruit in its trees and put fish in its lagoons. He freed the spirit Ariel from the split pine tree. He even tried to educate and civilize the monstrous Caliban until the task proved too hard. And all the time he waited. What was he waiting for? For rescue? Surely not, for though he had been Duke of Milan, here he was emperor of a magic realm.

Then one night, to Miranda's dismay, Prospero raised a storm. He pored over his books of spells, drew symbols in the sand, milked mysterious magic out of the clouds and, with Ariel's help, raised up such a tempest as the island had never seen before. The heaving sea holed the sky; the pitchy rain mottled the rocks; twisting palm leaves slashed the air to ribbons. Out at sea, a passing ship was ensnared in the storm's centre. Ariel charred it with lightning, clung to its masts in the shape of fire, split its canvas with hail, and blinded passengers and crew with rain. The ship was driven headlong against the cliffs, where it was held in a cleft as Ariel had been within his tree.

'Why, Father?' begged Miranda. 'Such a dreadful storm! All those poor people lost! Why would you do such a thing, Father?'

'I have my reasons,' said Prospero, allowing the wind to drop. 'And they're not all drowned. Take this young man coming towards us now, for instance. What do you make of him?'

Miranda looked down from the dripping doorway of their mountain cave and saw a young man roaming the island paths in a daze of grief. Every now and then, he would call out.

'Father! Father! Anyone! Is no one left alive, then, but me?'

'What is it, a god?' whispered Miranda, pressing her fingers to her mouth. 'He's so beautiful. Did you ever see such beauty, Father?' She was accustomed to the blue-green, feathered loveliness of Ariel, but this was nothing like it. This was flesh and blood. This was a wonder.

And yet Prospero did not welcome Ferdinand with sympathy and kindness. On the contrary, he was horribly fierce with him, accusing him of having come to the island expressly to steal it. A spy, he said, a treacherous dog fit for nothing but a kennel and a stout length of chain. When Ferdinand drew his sword to resist, Prospero's magic robbed him of all power to move, and though Miranda pleaded desperately on his behalf, Ferdinand was shackled like a convict and put to work carrying firewood.

Prince Ferdinand hardly cared. He had seen Miranda, miracle of the island, and she had looked back at him with the same love-struck eyes. Nothing else seemed to matter.

Ferdinand was wrong to think his father dead. Though Prospero (who had orchestrated every note of the storm) knew the truth, he did nothing to put the boy's mind at rest. Indeed, he had Ariel become invisible and sing sad songs of drowning in Ferdinand's ear.

But Ferdinand's father, King Alonso, was not dead. He and half the nobility of Naples and Milan were strewn round the island's shore, in accordance with Prospero's plan – soaked, exhausted, but alive. Among them was Prospero's deadly enemy Antonio.

King Alonso was devastated with grief, for he in turn believed his son had drowned. His companions – particularly Gonzalo – tried to comfort him by saying that Ferdinand could have swum ashore, but no one really believed it. Some were more sincere in their sympathy than others. For no sooner had the King and Gonzalo gone to sleep than Antonio resorted to his favourite pastime: plotting and murderous intrigue.

'If you were to kill Alonso now, while he's sleeping,' he whispered to Sebastian, 'and I were to put an end to that prig Gonzalo, you would go home from here King of Naples. You're heir to the throne, aren't you?'

'Me? Take Naples? Like you took Milan from your brother?'

'Yes, and how well his robes look on me!'

Sebastian hesitated. 'I don't know if I *could*. . . .'

'Nothing simpler,' urged Antonio, insidious and tempting. 'Three inches of steel – that's all that stands between you and the crown of Naples. Don't think about it. Let's just do it. . . .'

They could not know that every word spoken on the island rang loud in Prospero's ear. Quickly he sent Ariel to wake the victims, and Alonso and Gonzalo stirred in the nick of time to escape having their throats cut. The murderers' moment was lost; their crime had to be postponed, and the four went on searching for Alonso's lost son.

Meanwhile, Caliban the monster was busy cursing his miserable existence when he heard someone coming. He hid, for fear it was one of Prospero's spirits sent to punish his laziness with pinches. He lay down and hid – and that was how Trinculo and Stephano (two more survivors of the shipwreck) came upon him. Trinculo, Alonso's jester, looked round for shelter from a fresh burst of rain and, seeing Caliban's cloak, crept underneath it. Stephano, Alonso's butler, had stumbled across most of the island before he stumbled across Caliban. Owing to a lucky find – several bottles of wine washed ashore after the shipwreck – his brains were pretty much afloat in drink. Seeing what he took to be a two-headed, four-legged fairground freak, he generously slopped wine into the mouth at each end.

'Trinculo, this end is you!'

'Stephano, you're alive!'

'Can I have some more wine?' asked Caliban, and they both jumped out of their wits. So it was that two rogues were reunited – and Caliban discovered a taste for strong liquor. He thought it so marvellous that he was ready to bow down and worship the god-like creatures who gave it to him, ready to serve them with slavish devotion – to show them his island, to let them *have* it, if they would just kill Prospero first. His head reeled with the drink. His fish fins slapped like a performing seal's as he thought of dancing on Prospero's corpse. He should have known that every word spoken on the island could be heard by Prospero. Prospero sent Ariel to accompany the trio's drunken singing on pipe and drum, and the music impelled them to dance, like it or not, through thistles and thorns, pits and ponds up to their chins. Even so, he could not remove from their hearts the determination to kill Prospero and take his island from him.

'Please sit down and rest! I'll carry some of your logs! Let me! But please rest! You look so tired.'

'I'd rather my back broke under the strain! And anyway, how can I be tired when you are here to keep me company?'

Prospero smiled with delight as he watched, unseen, his daughter and Prince Ferdinand. It was impossible to tell which of them was the more in love, and nowhere in the world could you have found two more admirable young people together in one place. He had planned their meeting from the very beginning, and had treated Ferdinand so cruelly only to test his mettle and be sure of his worth.

Now he put an end to their distress, wrapped Ferdinand warmly in his arms, and granted his wish to marry the beloved Miranda. 'She will make you even happier than you suppose, boy. I've had her by me here for twelve years and I know her for the perfection she is.' Then he entertained his visitor as he would have liked to have done from the first, with hospitality and friendship, and with a 'masque' or play to celebrate their forthcoming marriage. Though it was an illusion acted out by shadows, a prettiness which faded like a rainbow after rain, Ferdinand and Miranda were enchanted.

Only Prospero could not derive any pleasure from his own magic. Inwardly he was seething with rage at the thought of Caliban – evil, ungrateful Caliban – urging along his worthless conspirators, bent on bloody murder. Together with Ariel, Prospero loosed the goblins of the island to kick and prick, pummel and pound the three drunkards. It was as if Prospero hated Caliban for being a hideous brute in his beautifully crafted paradise.

Ariel, the instrument of Prospero's revenge, began to feel sorry for his master's victims – not Caliban but the noblemen on whom Prospero was now wreaking revenge for his twelve years' exile. But he obediently carried out Prospero's instructions.

He prepared another masque, taunting Duke Antonio, King Alonso, Sebastian and Gonzalo with visions of banquets which disappeared before they could taste the food. He had Ariel trap them within a thicket of saplings, powerless to move, and forced to listen to their crimes

cried aloud through the tree-trunk bars of their cage. 'You, Antonio! You, Alonso! You, Sebastian! We know you! You are the sinners who usurped Duke Prospero and sent him and his little innocent daughter to their deaths in the heaving sea! You see, Alonso, how you have paid for the death of a child with the death of your own son? That's right, weep for your crimes!'

'Where are they now, Ariel?' Prospero asked.

'Where you told me to put them, master, and so miserable that, if I were human, I would take pity on them.'

'You would? Then so shall I, my faithful Ariel. I promised you your freedom if you served me loyally, didn't I?' At the mention of freedom the blue-green feathers fluttered like a seabird hovering over the sea. 'I shall keep my word soon. Release my enemies and bring them here.' With his staff Prospero drew a magic circle on the ground in which to pen them a while longer.

It was dawn. The first warmth of the day touched him and Prospero unfastened his magician's cloak at the throat. The mystical signs woven into its fabric glistened and flickered. His mane of white hair made him god-like as he stood overseeing his island kingdom. And yet he leaned heavily on his staff as he addressed one last time the spirits of the island.

'Goodbye to you, wraiths of the rockpools, you ghosts of the green sea, you woodland sprites. My magic has given me such mastery that I could eclipse the sun or waken the dead to dance. But all that is finished now. Men are not gods and if they try to be so, they become tyrants.'

He let the cloak fall from his shoulders. He broke his wizard's staff and, fetching his book of magic from the cave, he hurled it down into the sea. The spine burst, and its pages hovered on the rising air like a thousand gulls.

Ariel brought all Prospero's enemies within the magic circle. They looked up to see, white-maned and king-like,

on a high promontory, the man they had thought long
drowned in the sea.

'Prospero!?' they all gasped.

'Yes, Antonio, Alonso, Sebastian. I am Prospero, the
Duke of Milan you cast adrift on the open sea. I have
tormented you for it in body and mind. But now I forgive
you. All I require of you is the return of my dukedom.'

'Oh, it's yours!' exclaimed Alonso. 'Every brick and
pane of it. This last storm's taught me that a dukedom's
nothing to lose compared with a son.'

'You must be patient in your loss, Alonso,' said
Prospero sagely. 'I myself lost a daughter in last night's
storm, but I have resigned myself to the loss.'

'You did? Oh heavens! How?'

Then, seeing that Alonso was truly a changed man,
Prospero drew the curtain which hung across the mouth
of the cave. There sat Ferdinand and Miranda playing
chess! Alonso's amazement was matched only by
Miranda's when she looked up to see her empty world
suddenly populated by so many human faces.

Ariel, obedient to the last, lifted down the ship from its
cleft in the cliffs, and woke the sailors who, all the while,
had slept a magic sleep below decks. The voyage of the
Duke of Milan and King of Naples, interrupted by
the tempest, could safely continue.

Even Stephano and Trinculo, pinched and bruised, fell
aboard at the last moment and lay in the bilges howling.

Fair weather and a safe passage were the last gifts
Prospero was able to pluck out of the treasure chest of
magic. After that, all he could give Ariel was his freedom,
all he could give his daughter and son-in-law was his
blessing as a father, and all he could give his subjects in
the dukedom of Milan was the wisdom of an old man.

Caliban was left alone on his island. No one remained
to torture him with pinches or force him to carry

firewood. No one remained to call him vile and hideous. No one remained for him to curse or envy or hate. But there again, no lovely Miranda remained, no magic to paint the air with music; no one to blame for the day's disappointments; no one to rouse tempests out of the sea. No one at all.

Sometimes, in the blue-green season of the year, he would glimpse Ariel riding on a snatch of wind or somersaulting through circles of sea left by a tunny's tail. Perhaps he wept at the sight. Who can say? No one remains to tell us.

The best in classic and

Jane Austen

Elizabeth Laird

Roddy Doyle

Beverley Naidoo

Robert Swindells

George Orwell

Charles Dickens

Charlotte Brontë

Jan Mark

Anne Fine

Anthony Horowitz